GAY PRIDE

BOOKS BY WILLIAM J. MANN

Novels

The Men from the Boys

The Biograph Girl

Where the Boys Are

Nonfiction

*Wisecracker: The Life and Times of William Haines,
Hollywood's First Openly Gay Star*

*Behind the Screen: How Gays and Lesbians Shaped
Hollywood 1910–1969*

Edge of Midnight: The Life of John Schlesinger

GAY PRIDE

A Celebration of All Things Gay and Lesbian

William J. Mann

CITADEL PRESS
Kensington Publishing Corp.
www.kensingtonbooks.com

CITADEL PRESS BOOKS are published by

Kensington Publishing Corp.
850 Third Avenue
New York, NY 10022

First Printing: November 2004

10   9   8   7   6   5   4   3   2   1

Printed in the United States of America

Library of Congress Control Number: 2004106174

ISBN 0-8065-2563-0

Contents

GAY PRIDE

Introduction

When my editor, John Scognamiglio, asked me if I'd come up with a list of 101 reasons I was proud to be gay, I thought it would be easy. Sure enough, lots of ideas came to me, and even more rolled in when I started polling my partner, Dr. Tim Huber, and several of my friends. The hard part came in cutting them down to 101; you'll find me longing for a 102nd slot several times in the following list.

In collections like these, of course, there will always be disagreements. What about this? How could you omit that? I tried not to be American centric, remembering that the great big gay world extends across the globe, but my particular life experience cannot help but influence my choices. I hope this will serve as a springboard for lots of other ideas. The reasons for pride are truly endless.

1

The Great MGM Musicals

Singin' in the Rain. Easter Parade. Words and Music. Babes in Arms. Meet Me in St. Louis. For Me and My Gal. The Pirate. Ziegfeld Follies. Annie Get Your Gun. Show Boat. An American in Paris.

The list could go on and on, but you get the picture. All those great 1940s and '50s movie musicals came from gay talent. The Freed Unit at MGM has been widely hailed as the greatest musical-producing department in the entire studio era. While head honcho Arthur Freed wasn't gay himself, his unit was dubbed "Freed's Fairies." Everyone knew it was a powerhouse force of creative queens turning out these pictures, led by the inimitable Roger Edens, the same man who'd spotted the talent in a chubby little unknown girl named Frances Gumm and molded her into Judy Garland. Edens was responsible for some of the best musicals of all time: in addition to producing the above films, he also provided musical adaptations for *The Wizard of Oz* and *On the Town*, and on his own produced *Funny Face* and *Hello Dolly!*

Edens wasn't Freed's only fairy: there were also directors Charles

Walters and Vincente Minnelli (though the latter did his best to pretend otherwise), orchestral arranger Conrad Salinger, choreographers Robert Alton and Jack Cole, dancer and Freed assistant Don Loper, and many others. The Freed musicals revolutionized the genre by seamlessly integrating the musical and dance elements into the storyline—a heritage acknowledged as recently as the film version of *Chicago,* which also had a largely gay creative team behind it.

So next time one of these gems shows up on Turner Classic Movies, take a look. Observe the gay sensibility at work in the "Great Lady" sequence of *Ziegfeld Follies.* Listen to the texture and color in the orchestration of *Meet Me in St. Louis.* Watch Judy Garland turn gender roles upside-down in *Easter Parade.* The work of Freed's Fairies is indeed immortal.

2

Alexander the Great

Okay, so how are we supposed to be proud of a cutthroat invader who conquered most of Eurasia, sacked cities, sold folks into slavery, and casually whacked off people's heads with his sword? In truth, historians tend to view Alexander as one of the more benevolent of despots, enlightened for his time (which was, after all, circa 330 B.C.). He insisted on treating his conquered hordes with equanimity, often restoring the vanquished rulers to power. He rejected the Greek ideal that the Persians and other races were inferior barbarians, fit only for Greek domination. In fact, he integrated much of Persian culture into his court, even taking a Persian boy as a lover. He was known for his tolerance—allowing a degree of religious freedom in his empire—and had a deep and abiding respect for women. There was no harem chained by the ankles following Alexander's army.

Maybe that's because Alexander—king of Macedonia and conqueror of most of the world as then known—was too much in love with his boyhood friend Hephaestion to ever have time to rape and enslave women the way his contemporaries did. Now matter how current movies depict him, Alexander seems to have been predominately attracted to men. Both Alexander and Hephaestion had been tutored by Aristotle, with Alexander envisioning themselves as those two great heroes from Greek tradition, Achilles and Patroclus.

Most historians now accept that the relationship between Alexander and Hephaestion was romantic and sexual. While same-sex sexual relationships were a common and accepted part of the ancient world, these tended to end in adulthood with marriage to a woman. But Alexander and Hephaestion remained steadfast until the end—two adult men as companions and lovers, their relationship recognized by the world (much of which, of course, they ruled). Long after Alexander's death, the Cynic philosophers would say that he had been defeated just once in his life, and that was by Hephaestion's thighs.

3

Off-Off Broadway

You take it for granted now, all those naked boys singing and those strange edgy shows in coffeehouses where girls smear themselves with chocolate. But Off-Off Broadway hasn't always been an option for theatergoers. In the late 1950s and early '60s, an alternative theater movement arose, spearheaded by avant-garde artists like Judith Malina and Julian Beck—as well as one man whose name has become synonymous with bold, risk-taking theater: Joe Cino.

It was Cino who opened and gave his name to the Caffe Cino at 31 Cornelia Street in New York City's Greenwich Village in 1958—the birth of Off-Off-Broadway. The Cino influence on American theater cannot be exaggerated. Here such dramatists as Tom Eyen, John Guare, Robert Heide, William Hoffman, Harry Koutoukas, Doric Wilson, Robert Patrick, Sam Shepard, and Lanford Wilson got their start. And right from the beginning, Cino had an obvious gay influence, championed by the unapologetic, openly gay man at its head. Most of the artists who worked at the Cino were, in fact, gay men, friends of Joe's brought into the charged, creative atmosphere of the little theater. Ten years before Stonewall—and already a conscious, distinctly gay sensibility was being articulated in their work.

When Lanford Wilson's one-act about a drag queen in crisis, *The Madness of Lady Bright,* opened at the Caffe Cino in 1964, gay theater was born—followed a few months later by Robert Patrick's *The Haunted Host.* But what made Joe Cino's coffeehouse-theater so revolutionary—and lastingly influential—was his seamless integration of sensibilities, moving from Wilson's camp to the realism of Sam Shepard, transcending easy labels like gay and straight. Plays presented at the Cino ranged from reconsiderations of the classics to new, experimental plays and even to musicals: *Dames at Sea* ran for years Off-Broadway and made a star of Bernadette Peters.

Joe Cino's legacy was to ensure a place outside the safe, careful theater mainstream for work that dared to defy convention. The theater closed when Cino died in 1967—still two years before the supposed start of the American gay movement—but its influence remained, setting the stage (so to speak) for the Judson Poets Theatre, La Mama, and Charles Ludlum's Ridiculous Theater Company, all of which revitalized the New York theater scene by making sure fringe voices had a chance to be heard.

4

Ellen DeGeneres

Yep, she is. And with that simple acknowledgment Ellen DeGeneres changed forever the rules of Hollywood.

Actors have lived within the celluloid closet since movies first began flickering across the silver screens a century ago. Stonewall didn't make it easier for them, it just upped the ante. Actors knew their careers would be over if the media connected them to the burgeoning gay movement. The demands of activists for celebrities to "come out" only pushed them deeper into the closet. Gay and lesbian actors lived in a constant state of fear.

When Ellen came out—on one of the highest-rated episodes of a sitcom ever—she took a long sigh of relief, echoed by every actor who's taken the plunge since. Sure, it was a ratings grabber, though *Ellen* (the show) lasted only another season. But Ellen (the woman) had forever reset the parameters. Suddenly gay leads on TV shows were conceivable. *Ellen* begat *Will and Grace,* which begat the American *Queer as Folk.*

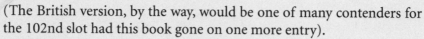

(The British version, by the way, would be one of many contenders for the 102nd slot had this book gone on one more entry).

Ellen paved the way for actors who continue to follow her lead (though they aren't exactly beating down the path). By refusing to live under the fear of exposure, Ellen threw off the yoke that had oppressed Richard Chamberlain and so many like him, and took charge of her career. Every celeb who's come out has said that it's made things easier, and none have said that it negatively impacted their careers. Though her TV series might come and go, it's clear Ellen is here to stay. Having Disney create a character just for you—a fish with short-term memory lapses in *Finding Nemo*—proves that. By simply being who she is—sharp, smart, funny, and oh, yeah, gay—Ellen DeGeneres is definitely reason to be proud.

5

Haute Couture

As Karen on *Will and Grace* once observed, stumbling upon a "conversion therapy" group: "They're trying to make gay people straight? Good Lord, don't they know what that'll do to the fall line?"

For more than a century, fashion design has been tucked, hemmed, altered, and shaped by gay men. Adrian, Erté, Travis Banton, Orry-Kelly, Howard Greer, Rudi Gernreich, Christian Dior, Cristobal Balenciaga, Bob Mackie, Jean-Paul Gaultier, Gianni Versace, Domenico Dolce, Stefano Gabbana—this is one list that truly just won't quit. Whether it's been Adrian's padded shoulders for Joan Crawford or Versace's body-conscious styles that redefined menswear, gay designers have set the trends the whole world copied.

Let's consider just a few of the hundreds. Halston was the first true international fashion superstar. That pill-box hat Jackie Kennedy wore at JFK's inauguration? Halston. Those sharp and slinky dresses popularized by Liza and Bianca at Studio 54? Halston. His elegance was imbued with a bold simplicity, creating a minimalist look based on conceptual art principles. His influence has proven timeless.

Then of course there's Yves Saint Laurent, one of the seminal fashion designers of the past century. He appropriated street fashion with his black leather jackets and knitted turtlenecks, and later he created the first female tuxedo. His androgynous creations, according to critics, feminized the basic shapes of the male wardrobe, establishing a whole new set of standards for world fashion.

Today we have, among so many others, Tom Ford, who revived Gucci with a much-needed dose of sexualized glamour. Ford led a revolution of sorts in the way men approach fashion. We've come to expect nothing less.

6

Cher

No, Cher isn't gay. But there are plenty of reasons gay folk can take pride when they look upon their favorite diva's career. When her farewell concert was recently televised, the camera kept turning to mobs of shrieking men mouthing along the lyrics to Cher's greatest hits. (Tell me how many straight men you know who can recite the words to "Half Breed.") There, on national television, was the key to understanding why Cher's career has lasted this long. It's because gay men love her.

Take nothing away from the lady's talent and drive. But gay men have had an eye on her since she first sashayed onto the stage on *The Sonny and Cher Comedy Hour* in those glittery Bob Mackie gowns. Cher had sass, she had style, she had great timing, and oh man, could she ever put down that little runt of a husband with just a saucy little swing of her hair. She could play a vamp (or a scamp, or a bit of a tramp) or Laverne the Launderette Lady, who wore leopard print tights and snapped her chewing gum. We marked her then as a keeper.

When daughter Chastity came out as a dyke, it all just seemed to fit:

of *course* Cher was going to be okay about it. She's practically one of us anyway, even if we like to forget the whole Gregg Allman thing. She's even acknowledged the debt she owes to her gay fans, saying "they've always been there." That's for sure: we even watched the infomercials. We just would not let this lady's career end. We would not allow her to be written off or forgotten. A few years ago, it was the gay clubs that first spun "Believe" into the mega-hit it became, ensuring yet another go-round for the diva who just won't die.

There will, of course, be some out there who will insist this is nothing to be proud of—that we should have, in fact, let our diva fade away into obscurity a long time ago. But we don't listen to them. We'll be dancing to a ninety-year-old Cher when we're sixty. Just watch.

7

The Ancient Greeks

What's there to be proud about the Ancient Greeks? Well, only that they set the groundwork for all of Western Civilization, thought up the concept of democracy, encouraged some of the most original thinking before or since, and oh, yeah: they actually celebrated same-sex love.

Homosexuality was simply a part of the broad spectrum of human relationships in ancient Greece, just one more facet of love and sexuality. Early Hellenic society enjoyed what some historians call a "nonexclusive heterosexuality"; bisexuality was taken for granted. In such a world, older men routinely welcomed eager, nubile youths to their beds and to their lives, mentoring them and teaching them and loving them. To the Greeks, the relationship between a man and a boy was the most pure form of love that existed.

The women of ancient times weren't left out either. The word *lesbian,* in fact, is derived from the Greek island of Lesbos, the birthplace of Sappho (who lived around 600 B.C.). Sappho was a priestess of a feminine love cult. She celebrated the love of women for women in her poems and other writings, still read today. Remember those old comic books with Wonder Woman uttering the line "Suffering Sappho"? They take on a whole new meaning. (The Amazing Amazon gets her own entry—check it out.)

Other great poets and philosophers of Ancient Greece also celebrated their same-sex relationships. These include Anacrean (563–478 B.C.), Euripedes (480–406 B.C.), Sophocles (496–406 B.C.), Socrates (470–399 B.C.), and Plato (427–347 B.C.). From philosophy to law to democracy to literature, the world is indebted to the ancient Greeks, from whom same-sex love was a defining part of existence. Might I go so far then as to say homosexuality formed the very building blocks of our society? Sappho and Socrates and Plato wouldn't disagree.

8

Will and Grace

It's gotten trendy lately to not like this show. When it first came on, of course, everyone loved it—queens were riffing off it over watercoolers all across North America. But somewhere along the line the conventional wisdom became: *It's over. It doesn't go far enough. It's all a big cartoon.*

I'm reminded of GLAAD's (Gay & Lesbian Alliance Against Defamation) infamous press release of a few years back, when they tried to whip up outrage that there were only like, I don't know, *thirty-seven* gay and lesbian characters on television. I'm old enough to remember—heck, my twelve-year-old niece is old enough to remember—when a same-sex kiss on *Roseanne* caused a national uproar. Things have changed since then. Do we still have a ways to go? Of course. But television took a light-year leap into the future on September 21, 1998, the night *Will and Grace* debuted.

I mean, this is American national television with dialogue like this:

WILL: *(playing cards with Grace)* Grace, you should know better. In this house, a queen beats a straight every time!

WILL: You're just not my type of woman. I prefer . . . someone taller. And, uh, with a hairy chest.

Thanks to the inspiration of openly gay creator Max Mutchnick and the brilliant writing staff—gay, straight, whatever, but all inspired by a gay sensibility—the wit and wisdom of homo culture is being brought into America's living rooms.

A whole generation is growing up who will remember Will Truman and Jack McFarland as fond friends—much the way an earlier generation recalls Rob Petrie and Barney Fife. Yes, Will needs a regular sex life, but still, every Thursday night, *W&G* makes sure that gay life will never again be hidden in the closet.

JACK: Tonight I'm supervising an event at the Waldorf-Astoria. I will have eight men under me. How great is that?

WILL: Eight men? What'd you do, write the Gay Make A Wish Foundation?

9

Eleanor Roosevelt

She was called the "First Lady to the World." And indeed Eleanor Roosevelt has left a lasting imprint on history, one of the true giants of the twentieth century. Her long relationship with journalist Lorena Hickok—beautifully documented in a series of poignant, intimate love letters—gave her the emotional grounding she needed after the devastation of discovering her husband's affair with Lucy Mercer.

Roosevelt was one of those rare souls for whom concern for humankind was truly the driving force of her life. During the Great Depression, she established schools for poor children and organized factories for the unemployed. Many of her ideas were incorporated into the president's New Deal social programs. Eleanor knew some of the country considered her an "interfering woman"—though that hardly kept her at home baking cookies. She offered an inspiration to a generation: Hillary Clinton didn't appear out of nowhere.

Her daily newspaper-syndicated column, "My Day," challenged Americans in soft, folksy wisdom to rethink their outdated notions and biases—

a goal that's been sadly inverted today, when the spin out of politics seems to be lulling Americans into complacency with the status quo. Yet Eleanor just couldn't comprehend politics without compassion. Outraged by the rampant discrimination faced by African Americans, Eleanor badgered her husband until he signed executive orders ensuring equal treatment in the various New Deal projects. In 1938, while attending the Southern Conference for Human Welfare in Birmingham, she flouted segregation by sitting with the black attendees. And the following year, in a very public gesture, she resigned from the Daughters of the American Revolution after that group had barred Marian Anderson from its auditorium.

After her husband's death in 1945, Eleanor served as American spokesperson at the United Nations, where she helped found UNICEF and chaired the Human Rights Commission. Eleanor Roosevelt's life was informed by choices of courage and integrity. She recognized that in her position she could either be a smiling, background presence to her husband's ambitions, or she could use her visibility and influence to make a difference, transform society, and help humankind evolve. This moral commitment is sadly missed today.

10

ACT UP

They were a group of angry young men and women, some infected with HIV, others not. Some were raging over the deaths of loved ones; others were facing the obscene realization that—at ages when they should have been thinking of buying homes or getting ahead in their careers—they would need to start planning their funerals and drawing up wills.

And the government shrugged. In eight years in office, while thousands died, Ronald Reagan never once uttered the word *AIDS*. The most his successor, the first President Bush, ever did was permit his wife to put a candle in the window of the White House as part of a vigil.

No wonder people were angry. No wonder they took to the streets. The AIDS Coalition to Unleash Power held its first action on Wall Street to protest the profiteering of pharmaceutical companies with AIDS-related drugs. Traffic was snarled and windows were broken, but that was just the beginning. In the years to come, an open coffin was carried from Washington Square to the New York Republican Party HQ. Blood was spilled on the White House lawn. Mass was disrupted at St. Patrick's Cathedral.

There had never been anything like it before. ACT UP was media savvy, knowing how to get the news cameras to show up and the headline writers to use their language. ACT UP shamed the world's most powerful nation into finally recognizing the health crisis at hand. Some called ACT UP just a bunch of crybabies. But those crybabies helped accomplish needle exchange, condom distribution, sex education in schools, increased public spending for research and prevention, the reform of insurance laws, and the Americans with Disabilities Act.

And they did it with style. Just think of some of the daring, provocative artists and writers associated with ACT UP: Larry Kramer, Vito Russo, Keith Haring, Robert Mapplethorpe, Sarah Schulman, Mike Signorile. They changed the world. While the fight remains, we are getting close to the time that Vito Russo imagined when he inspired his comrades by saying, "Remember that someday the AIDS crisis will be over. And when that day has come and gone there will be people alive who will hear that once there was a terrible disease, and that a brave group of people stood up and fought and in some cases died so that others might live and be free."

11

Chicago

They said it couldn't be done. Reinventing the movie musical for the 2000s. Impossible. No one will sit still long enough. No one will put up with people breaking into song in the middle of the scene. It can't be done.

They were wrong. And a gaggle of gay men proved it.

Chicago won the Best Picture Academy Award for 2002. And deservedly so. The award should go to that film which pushed the boundaries of cinema, that redefined form or structure. And *Chicago* did just that with eye-popping style—courtesy of gay director Rob Marshall, gay screenwriter Bill Condon, and gay executive producers Craig Zadan and Neil Meron. If any movie can be said to be a gay product, this one can.

Attempts to turn the Broadway show *Chicago* into a movie had been made for more than a decade. But always there was the same problem: how does a stage musical—especially one where the songs advance the plot and give depth to the characters—translate to the screen for today's audiences? The stage is granted a certain suspension of the ordinary rules of behavior. Audiences tolerate the idea of Roxy Hart turning from a "real-time" conversation with her husband or lawyer and launching into a song about her dreams and ambitions. And in the old days, movie audiences did the same: Judy Garland could croon "Have Yourself a Merry Little Christmas" to Margaret O'Brien, accompanied by a full orchestra in her backyard, and no one batted an eye.

But in an era when we accept without much trouble Charlie's Angels landing on their high-heeled feet after a plunge off a ten-story building, we seem to turn our noses up at the idea of a song. So Bill Condon—already a reason for pride for his beautiful film *Gods and Monsters*—came up with a deceptively simple solution: the musical numbers would be fantasy sequences, all directed, staged, and cut with the pizzazz of an MTV video. And it worked—brilliantly. Audiences flocked to see *Chicago*, and the movie musical was reborn for the new century.

12

The Culinary Revolution

I'm sure you all have at least one friend who's a dynamo in the kitchen, who invites you to dinner and always serves the trendiest *aps* (that's what they're calling appetizers these days) and the perfectly chosen wine. It's no surprise that gay and lesbian chefs were vital in the culinary revolution of the 1990s. For a group of people who idolized Julia Child while still in training pants—and who would go on to adopt Martha Stewart as their patron saint (just count all the "Free Martha" stickers in gay ghettos)—this is hardly breaking news.

Among the gay stars of the culinary revolution have been Gary Danko, who presides over the world-famous Dining Room at the Ritz Carlton in San Francisco, and Susan Feniger, the "lesbian half" of the popular Food Network cooking show. With her cooking partner Mary Sue Milliken, Feniger also runs Border Grill and Ciudad in Los Angeles, and the Border Grill at the Mandalay Hotel and Casino in Las Vegas.

But you don't have to go high-end. Gay neighborhoods are now known as havens of good cooking; straight tourists often flock to the

Castro or West Hollywood or Chelsea or Dupont Circle because they know they'll find some of the trendiest, hippest, most exciting and best-tasting restaurants in the city.

And it's not just the food but the aesthetics of the presentation. Remember what meals looked like in the 1970s and '80s? There were meat, potatoes and vegetables, served as if in a TV dinner: the meat occupying the lower half of the plate, the starch and the greens in each of the upper two quarters. Now we've got edible flowers like orchids and pansies and lilacs decorating the tops, and entire sculptures of rosemary branches and chives reaching up toward the ceiling. Dining has become a feast not only for the taste buds but also for the senses of sight and smell. So next time you have dinner at the home of one of your fabulous chef friends, remember to thank him or her for being part of a sensibility that changed the world.

13

Dorothy Allison

Born in Greenville, South Carolina, Dorothy Allison is one of the finest writers of her generation. There are few works of literature that rise to the heights of *Bastard Out of Carolina,* a finalist for the National Book Award in 1992. Allison also penned the best seller *Cavedweller,* another evocative slice of her heart and mind, as well as a chapbook of her performance work, *Two or Three Things I Know for Sure.*

Her brilliance as an artist alone is enough to include her among the reasons I'm proud to be gay. But many extraordinary gay writers deserve admiration for their sheer talent. Dorothy Allison's artistry transcends the written word: she has a soul connection to humanity like few others. A mentor to many younger writers, including myself, Allison founded the Independent Spirit Award, a prize given each year to an individual whose work with small presses and independent bookstores has helped sustain these important traditions.

Here's a story that says it all. A couple of years ago, in a lecture at Stanford University, Allison considered the meaning of freedom. "You're in a lifeboat," she pondered. "The wind is rising. The sea is rising. There are nineteen others in the boat, too, but it can only hold twelve safely. What do you do?"

She remembered being issued that same challenge in college. Her classmates had struggled with the ethics, some of them breaking down into tears.

"Is this not truly how our lives are constructed?" Allison asked her audience. "Who gets to go to school? Who gets invited to a small, special institution [and] told they have the possibility of genius? Who gets nurtured—led along and encouraged and shaped? Who has to stay home and watch the babies while Mama cleans houses? Who gets a scholarship? Who does not? Is it a lifeboat we live in?"

"It *is* a lifeboat," she told the crowd. "It's your life. It's a nation. You are a citizen. You are good enough to put one hand out and take the arm of the other. The wind's rising, the boat's bouncing, the water's coming in. Some of us will have to hang over the side. Some of us will have to paddle. Because none of us is going down while I'm here. I'm giving up nobody."

14

Gay Soldiers

I'm not a big fan of military culture. It's often dehumanizing and sexist, and homophobia is ingrained into its very core. In the United States, the military has been used to do things for which I am certainly not proud, from dropping the atomic bomb to burning Vietnamese villages to waging an illegal war on Iraq.

But soldiers, on the other hand—soldiers and sailors and marines—the individual men and women who fought for our country's independence, who died on the fields of Europe to stop the spread of fascism, who continue to risk their lives every day—invoke great admiration and pride.

And I take particular pride in the gay and lesbian servicepeople among them, who have defended their country while at the same time being forced to defend themselves from hateful, traitorous supposed comrades. President Clinton tried to make it easier for them to serve with dignity and honesty, but the resulting policy was a horrible parody of the original intent. At this writing—even while gays serve openly and without problem in the militaries of Canada, Britain, Israel, and others—gay U.S. servicemen and -women are still routinely hounded, harassed, and discharged dishonorably.

And still they serve. Still they do what they have pledged to do.

Let's remember Leonard Matlovich, a hero of the Vietnam War, less famous now for his heroics than for his fight with the Air Force to recognize his right to serve as an openly gay person in the military. Let's remember Colonel Margarethe Cammermeyer, a highly decorated nurse who had received the Bronze Star, who bravely turned her discharge into a cause *celebre* until a federal judge ordered her reinstatement in 1994. Let's remember Perry Watkins, the first gay African American serviceperson to challenge the ban. Let's remember Barry Winchell and Allen Schindler, who were killed by colleagues who resented their refusal to conform to heterosexual norms. Let's remember all of those who are out there today. Reasons for pride? Absolutely.

15

Sir Ian McKellen

Gandalf is gay. How cool is that? So is Magneto. That information eventually filters down to all those adolescents watching and cheering *The Lord of the Rings* trilogy or the various *X-Men* films—and you know what? They don't care. They cheer him on just the same. The world is changing, and it's due in no small part to people like Sir Ian.

McKellen's career began in the English theater, where being gay was commonplace, even routine, to those in the know. But such things weren't talked about, and an earlier generation saw no reason why they ever should be. But McKellen was a young man who moved with the changes he saw happening in the world. In 1988, he came out publicly on the BBC *Radio 4* program in response to Margaret Thatcher's "Section 28," that barbaric piece of legislation that made the "public promotion of homosexuality" a crime. It was reason enough for McKellen to take a stand, and he has been active in the gay movement ever since.

A brilliant actor, he has seen his career skyrocket. Whether playing

James Whale in the film *Gods and Monsters*, various Shakespearean roles, or his latest fantasy heroes, McKellen consistently surprises and delights audiences with his range. In 1990, he was knighted by Queen Elizabeth.

McKellen is proof that one can be out and still be a roaring success. He founded the gay-rights group Stonewall UK, and his one-man show, *A Knight Out*, performed all over the world, has benefited various gay organizations. The heights of his career have yet to be scaled by Sir Ian McKellen, and he will reach them as an outspoken, proud gay man.

16

Billy Budd

Herman Melville's greatest contribution to literature is, of course, *Moby Dick*—one of the finest novels ever written, one of the true masterpieces of Western culture. But perhaps more beautiful, more haunting, more challenging, is *Billy Budd, Sailor,* and only those with their heads still stuck in the sand can deny that it was written by a man consumed with same-sex desire. This is a novella of great power, taught in schools and analyzed endlessly by critics. In fact, writer David Greven has observed that finding the meaning of Melville's *Billy Budd* has become a sort of "initiation rite" within theory and criticism culture. This novella is enigmatic and bewitching, filled with apparently unsolvable riddles. And it is the result of a homosexual man's fascination with the homosocial world, inspired and informed by his homosexual passion for beautiful young men.

Billy Budd is the "Handsome Sailor," a main motif of the novella and an archetype that has endured both in gay and mainstream culture. Paul Cadmus, Tom of Finland, Abercrombie & Fitch—the images are readily at hand. What makes *Billy Budd* so important, however, what gives it such a lasting influence on the culture, is its central moral question: Did Captain Vere make the right choice in condemning Billy to death? As one critic framed the dilemma: Was Billy Budd a final concession to the forces of jurisprudence, social control, and rationalism—a conservative testament of status quo? Or was it, rather, an indictment of the dehumanization of man in a "civilized" era, a work of bitter irony—not conservative at all, but a radical testament of resistance?

It is exactly that kind of ambiguous debate that turns a novel into an enduring work of art. *Billy Budd* poses some of the most difficult questions with which society must contend, and for which there are no easy, unqualified answers.

17

Alan Turing

The founder of computer science, a brilliant mathematician, philosopher, wartime codebreaker, visionary—here was an unapologetic gay man well ahead of his time. In 1936, Alan Turing invented what was called "the Turing machine"—in effect, the concept for the world's first computer.

Now don't expect to fully understand what I'm about to say. I'm not even sure I do. But Turing's brilliance went something like this: the concept of "the Turing machine," like that of any *formula* or *equation,* is that an infinite number of Turing machines are possible, each corresponding to a different algorithm. That much a number of people had already figured out. But Turing perceived that if each particular algorithm was written out as instructions in standard form, the work of interpreting those instructions would, in and of itself, be a mechanical process, and so could then be incorporated into any other Turing machine—hence, the idea of the *Universal* Turing machine, the foundation of computer science. A Universal Turing machine could be made to do what any other Turing machine could do, simply by giving it the standard form. Hence: one machine for all conceivable tasks. We call it a computer.

Yet what's more impressive is that Turing conjured up this fundamental possibility right out of his mathematical imagination, because computers did not exist in 1936. Only a decade later would electronic technology catch up with Turing's mind, making it possible to apply his ideas to actual engineering.

During World War II, Turing turned his beautiful mind toward cryptanalytic efforts to decode the Enigma, the German's secret language. Thrilled to take on a problem that had stumped others, Turing managed to crack the code, ensuring victory in the Battle of the Atlantic.

Brilliant, heroic, insightful—but still Turing was arrested, in 1952 (in that wonderful decade) for the "crime" of being a homosexual. Stripped of his security clearance, his work declined along with his reputation. Alan Turing, to whom every user of Windows, e-mail, or digital cameras owes an incalculable debt, killed himself with cyanide in 1954.

18

The Member of the Wedding

Carson McCullers caused a literary sensation when she was just twenty-three years old, when her first novel, *The Heart Is a Lonely Hunter,* was published. It was quickly determined that this strange little girl-boy was not the typical "lady author," but rather an artist of excruciating detail. "She could evoke," as one critic wrote, "a vision of existence as terrible as it is real," whose narratives force us to encounter the depths of the spiritual and emotional isolation that are, ultimately, the foundation for the human condition."

But, as brilliant as all her work is, McCullers' keenest pride must come from *The Member of the Wedding,* the achingly heartfelt story of little Frankie Adams, a twelve-year-old boy-girl—a transgendered teen well before the term was coined—who must deal with the raging adolescent feelings that threaten to consume her as her family prepares for the wedding of her older brother.

The novel (published in 1945), the play (1951), and the film (1952) of *The Member of the Wedding* are all ruminations on loneliness and difference. Frankie's pain as an awkward, atypical girl is reflected in the life of her cook, played memorably by Ethel Waters on the stage. The loneliness that beats at the heart of the story, however, is tempered by the undefeated imagination of Frankie, leaving room for hope. McCullers, for all her own eccentricity, loved humanity. John Mason Brown wrote that *The Member of the Wedding* was "plainly the work of an artist and an author who does not stoop to the expected stencils, one who sees people with her own eyes rather than through borrowed spectacles."

As a woman who loved both men and women in her lifetime, McCullers is difficult to label, and we shouldn't try. Sarah Schulman came closest when she said she thought of McCullers as *transgendered,* and given the depiction of Frankie, that seems to make sense. What's unquestioned is McCullers' essential *queerness,* of being apart from the rest, different—a perspective that allowed her to offer some of the most beautiful and heartbreaking insights into the human condition ever put into words or acted on a stage.

19

Michelangelo's *David*

The pinnacle of Michelangelo's genius emerged from a plain block of used marble, eighteen feet tall, ruined (so everyone thought) by the hackings of another sculptor. Well known for his love affairs with the beautiful young (male) models who posed for him, Michelangelo was incredibly ambitious, determined to create a work of art that would get him noticed. His choice to create a colossal tribute to the male form should come as no surprise. (After all, his twenty nude youths in the Sistine Chapel would later scandalize the pope, for they were clearly more Greek than Christian in their ideal, playing no role in the religious narrative. They were simply eye candy.)

Chisel in hand, Michelangelo began the process of sculpting the marble into the familiar statue that has become an enduring symbol of Western art. Consider the effort that was needed, however. Michelangelo had to work around all the marks and cuts the last sculptor had made—in carving marble he couldn't just slap on new material as one might with clay. He had to be extremely precise, absolutely certain of every single slice of his chisel.

The result is magnificent: David, just after defeating Goliath, his catapult swung nonchalantly over his shoulder. He stands in classic pose, a testament to youth and beauty. What made the statue such an immediate sensation was its height, a considerable achievement in fifteenth-century Florence. But it was more than that. In *David*, Michelangelo had achieved the perfect blend of realism and idealism. There might be veins standing out in his right hand, sinews obvious in his turned neck—but he is also the image of man perfected. He is Adam before the Fall.

The great sixteenth-century art historian Vasari declared, "To be sure, anyone who has seen Michelangelo's *David* has no need to see anything else by any other sculptor, living or dead."

20

The Castro

Okay, so a Pottery Barn has opened up at the corner of Castro and Market, and some longtime residents decry the spike in rental costs and the creeping suburban gentrification. But it remains true that for any first-time gay visitor, alighting off the trolley at that famous intersection is like stepping into Oz.

The gay community in San Francisco developed after World War II, when thousands of gay military personnel, both men and women, returned to the United States through the port of San Francisco. Many chose to stay in the city rather than go back to repressive small towns in the East and Midwest. By the mid-1970s, the gay neighborhood had emerged as a political power, and it was from here that Harvey Milk ran for supervisor.

What the Castro came to signify for many gay and lesbian people all across the country was home—a place where they could live openly, love freely, and speak plainly. It was a magnet for those who had been rejected by their families, for all the disaffected and the disillusioned from small, conservative towns. The Castro drew the misfits and the make-believers, creating a fantasy world that was gloriously real, a place where freedom and tolerance thrived.

The Castro birthed the rainbow flag, the Different Light chain of bookstores, the Sisters of Perpetual Indulgence, the AIDS Memorial Quilt. During the AIDS crisis, the Castro taught by example how a community takes care of its own. Here the blueprint for advocacy organizations was made, from Project Inform to Gay Men's Health Crisis, publicizing information treatments and prevention. The hedonism of the 1970s—with all its bars and discos and sex clubs and bathhouses—may have been tamped down a bit, but it never really disappeared. Today the sexual underground of San Francisco is still among the most vibrant in the world.

While today there are many vibrant gay places, the Castro remains the most famous gay neighborhood in the world. Historian Susan Stryker has called it "the symbolic main street of the city's queer community and an emblem of gay pride around the world." It has become synonymous with liberation, freedom, and celebration. And while critics point to rising prices and the problems of the homeless to prove it is no Shangri-la, the Castro retains an enduring place in the hearts of gay men and lesbians worldwide.

21

The NEA Four

Tim Miller, John Fleck, Holly Hughes, and Karen Finley—two gay men, a lesbian, and a queer-identified straight woman. Miller was known to get naked on stage and mouth off at the government for oppressing gay people and ignoring the AIDS epidemic. Fleck's show was called *Dirt*, in which he delighted in revealing the dirt and grime of society's underbelly. Hughes confronted the fears of both the Left and the Right, skewering hypocrisy with sarcasm and feminist wit. And Finley—well, she smeared herself with chocolate as if it were excrement while railing against the homophobic, racist patriarchy.

It was enough to get some members of Congress, particularly Jesse Helms, in quite the tizzy, so in June 1990, the four grants that would have gone to these artists were vetoed by NEA chief John Frohnmayer. They were singled out, it was made plain, because of their sexual orientation and political discourses, and despite the fact that all had been recommended for awards by the NEA peer review panel.

Clearly the NEA Four—as they came to be known in the press—

were being made examples of, lessons on what not to do if one wanted government funding. The arts were being sterilized for mass public consumption. It became a much larger issue than just the denial of four grants, taking on First Amendment implications.

Through it all, the four artists at the heart of the controversy remained true to their visions, though it wasn't always easy. Their messages—daring to criticize the government and remind people about such things as social justice, equality, and fairness—rang loud and clear. Even in the face of such censorship, the NEA Four remained committed to the basic core beliefs that had gotten them into trouble in the first place.

Although eventually they won a settlement where the government paid them the amount of the defunded grants and all their court costs, the forces of oppression weren't done with Miller, Fleck, Hughes, and Finley yet. In 1998, the Supreme Court decided to overturn part of Miller's case, determining that "standards of decency"—a vague and imprecise term if ever there was one—remain constitutional criterion for federal funding of the arts. Miller, for his part, has vowed to continue fighting for freedom of expression for fierce diverse voices.

22

The Bloomsbury Set

Sometimes magic happens when people come together. They call it *synergy*—a meeting of minds, souls, and hearts, when great things emerge from the communal association of dynamic people. In the early years of the twentieth century, such magic occurred in the London neighborhood of Bloomsbury, in the home of sisters Vanessa and Virginia Stephen.

The Stephen home quickly developed a reputation as a salon for artists and writers, brilliant young intellectual contemporaries of the sisters. It is remarkable how many were gay and lesbian, and indeed, how a queer sensibility and aesthetic helped shape the work of the Bloomsbury set. At various times, the group included historian Lytton Strachey, economist John Maynard Keynes, writers Clive Bell and E. M. Forster, and artists Duncan Grant and Roger Fry.

But their intellectual and spiritual heart was Virginia Stephen, who became Virginia Woolf when she married Leonard Woolf in 1912. Woolf's work—*Mrs. Dalloway, A Room of One's Own, The Waves,* and many others—established her as one of the twentieth century's great literary voices. Although she loved her husband, Virginia's great love was Vita Sackville-West, who inspired Woolf's classic of queer fantasy fiction *Orlando*.

Woolf may be the most renowned of the Bloomsbury set, but those witty, sparkling salons also produced some of the century's greatest figures of arts and letters, most of whom were not traditionally heterosexual. Lytton Strachey was acclaimed for revolutionizing the genre of biography by treating his subjects with wit and irony. John Maynard Keynes left an indelible imprint on economics, so much so that the thirty-year boom in Western industrial countries (circa 1945–1975) has often been called "the Age of Keynes." E. M. Forster's *Maurice* gets its own entry in this book.

The Bloomsbury set lost much of its heart and soul when Virginia Woolf drowned herself in 1941, though some of the members continued meeting informally into the 1950s. Yet their lasting contributions remain, an extraordinary source of pride for gay artists and thinkers—and anyone who dares imagine outside the box.

23

Maurice

I admit I saw the movie before I read the book. That's largely because, for decades, E. M. Forster's great ode to homo love was kept away from the eyes of the world—including budding young gay boys like me who needed it most. It's the story of an ordinary guy—okay, so an upper-class, privileged, ordinary guy—who just so happens to be gay in Edwardian England, back when the "buggeries" of Oscar Wilde were still within living memory. Lots of books of the time featured homosexual characters, but none were as self-affirming about it as Maurice Hall. Most went off and killed themselves or died long, lingering deaths of loneliness, but Forster wrote Maurice as the most sane and grounded and well-adjusted figure in the book.

When he took pen to paper in 1912 to write *Maurice*, Forster knew he was directly challenging the status quo. What if a lad didn't *want* to get married? What if after he left school he *still* wanted to boink boys? Could he be happy? Or was he doomed?

A visit to the poet Edward Carpenter and his lover, a working-class

Derbyshire bloke named George Merrill, inspired Forster to end *Maurice* on a happy note. Our hero rejects the capitulation of his university lover and instead finds bliss with Alec Scudder, the gamekeeper on his country estate. Forster would later write that although such a happy ending was probably not plausible, he just couldn't bear to give the novel a disastrous finale. He packed it away in a drawer, tacking on a note to his future executors: "Publishable—but worth it?"

Indeed it was, for in 1971, when *Maurice* was finally given a posthumous publication, it was instantly proclaimed a literary classic. It is a poignant, articulate plea for emotional and sexual authenticity. It is also one of the great love stories, a work of tremendous romantic power, regardless of the protagonist's sexual orientation. Yes, we can take pride in its spirit of homo liberation, but we can also be proud of its tender, beautiful language and its fearless exploration of the human soul.

24

Blanche Dubois

Blanche Dubois is one the great characters of literature, and she is more a gay man than a real woman. Certainly she is completely, 100 percent, the creation of a gay male psyche, molded from a gay male experience. Tennessee Williams once said that "symbols are nothing but the natural speech of drama . . . the purest language of plays." Blanche is definitely a symbol—not only of Williams's repressed gayness, but of the overarching loneliness of humanity. In this he has created a lasting, indelible figure onto which we project our own longing, our own abandoned dreams.

It's not hard to see the gay genesis of the character. Blanche is a thirty-something woman, cast out of her village as if she were Hester Prynne. Indeed, her sexual misbehavior is what caused her current shame, though Blanche arrives at her sister's house armed with a false (yet easily shattered) air of haughtiness and sophistication. Blanche's backstory is vital to understanding the character: when she found her fiancé in bed with an older man, she had insulted him savagely, prompting his suicide. Her life since then has been a search to ease the ache in her soul. She is compelled to seduce young men, hopping from boy to boy, bed to bed.

With dialogue at turns poignant, bitter, sassy, and smart—but always eloquent and beautiful—the play is a gift to the English language. Blanche's famous line, "I have always depended upon the kindness of strangers," evokes so much, suggesting not only her own particular story but the stories of all of us, all of humanity, when we are vulnerable, lost, or alone. Blanche might live with self-delusion, keeping the lamps shaded to hide her true self, but we empathize with her. She has failed society and been cast off, and most of us—gay or straight—have known that experience at one time or another. When Stanley rapes her, it is more than violent, more than obscene. It is the victory of the brutish over the meek, the killing of a doe by a bear.

Few plays offer such insights into the human condition, and few characters in all of literature evoke so much empathy as Blanche Dubois.

25

P-FLAG

In 1972, a young man named Morton Manford was physically attacked at a gay rights demonstration in New York. At home, Morty's parents, Jeanne and Jules Manford, witnessed the attack on a local TV newscast. In utter horror they watched as the police failed to intervene and save their son. The outrage they experienced that day morphed them into activists—Super Mom and Super Dad. Thus began the Justice League of Homo America—otherwise known as Parents and Friends of Lesbians and Gays, or P-FLAG.

Every year at Gay Pride parades throughout North America, P-FLAG gets the loudest applause. That's because they are the only oppressed group *related* to their oppressors, and when families stand up to support them, they are breaking down the very structure of that oppression. A year after watching her son beaten on television, Jeanne Manford marched with him in New York's Pride Day parade. So many people ran up to her during the parade, imploring her to talk to their parents, that Jeanne decided to begin a support group. The first formal meeting of P-FLAG—then simply called Parents of Gays—took place in March 1973 at a local church. Approximately twenty people attended. Within a decade it had grown into a national organization with dozens of chapters.

Their mission statement says it all: "We, the parents, families and friends of lesbian, gay, bisexual, and transgendered persons, celebrate diversity and envision a society that embraces everyone, including those of diverse sexual orientations and gender identities. Only with respect, dignity, and equality for all will we reach our full potential as human beings, individually and collectively."

Of all the national organizations that work tirelessly on behalf of changing the world for gays, I'm proudest of P-FLAG. We love you, Mom and Dad.

26

Harvey Milk

Harvey Milk was the owner of a camera store in the Castro when he decided to run for the San Francisco Board of Supervisors. Today it might not seem like such a radical act; gay folk run for elected office all the time, and many win. There are congresspeople and mayors, and local city boards are loaded with gays and lesbians. But in 1977 being openly gay and running for office seemed incompatible. This was the stuff people got blackmailed about; what voter would listen to a pansy?

Milk wasn't the first to make the attempt: Frank Kameny ran for Congress from the District of Columbia in 1971, coming in fourth among six candidates, and Elaine Noble actually won a seat in the Massachusetts State House in 1974. (Both are top contenders, by the way, for that elusive 102nd spot.) But Milk's victory proved historic, for it engendered a huge swelling of gay pride (and gay political clout) in San Francisco and thereby ratcheted up gay visibility all across the nation. His sponsorshop of a "dog poop" ordinance got him national attention. It was a clever stunt. "All over the country, they're reading about me," he said, "and the story doesn't center on me being gay. It's just about a gay person who is doing his job."

Milk's victory had national implications. His campaign had been aimed at young gay people throughout the country as much as San Francisco voters. "You gotta give them hope," was Milk's motto, a mantra revived during Pride celebrations today.

In 1978, both Milk and San Francisco mayor George Moscone were shot and killed by former city supervisor Dan White. At his trial, White pleaded temporary insanity caused by too many additives in his fast-food diet. The media called it the "Twinkie defense," but it worked, with murder charges being reduced to manslaughter. On that day, the gay community rioted, overturning and burning police cars in a night of rage. Milk's murder galvanized as many—perhaps more—gay people as his election had. Having lived with death threats, Milk often spoke of his possible assassination. "If a bullet should enter my brain," he said, "let that bullet destroy every closet door."

27

Marches on Washington

Harvey Milk often imagined an enormous gay march on the nation's capital and spoke of it many times before his assassination in 1978. Soon after his death, inspired in part by his vision, the first National March on Washington for Lesbian and Gay Rights was held on October 14, 1979. Tens of thousands streamed into Washington, filling the Mall with chants of "Gay Power Now!"

The second gay March on Washington was held on October 11, 1987. Rev. Jesse Jackson was one of the first politicians to defy conventional wisdom and address the crowd. Organizers estimated 500,000 participants; two days after the march, 600 people were arrested at a demonstration of civil disobedience at the Supreme Court. Remember, in those days, the sodomy laws were still on the books.

The third march took place on April 25, 1993. The AIDS Quilt was also displayed on the Mall, stretching for acres, one of the most potent visual symbols of the epidemic. Nearly one million people took part.

The latest march, dubbed "The Millennium March," was held on

April 30, 2000. Not as many people this time—maybe half a million— but both President Clinton and Vice President Gore addressed the crowd on the Mall via video.

There's always some hullabaloo over these marches. Not enough of this, too much of that. Should they simply be about visibility, or should there be a specific political message? Ideological activists will always find a reason to get into a squabble, but in the end, at least where the Marches on Washington are concerned, that's beside the point. What has emerged from every march is a sense of empowerment. A sense of destiny. Marchers take back home with them the spirit of the march: a sense of community and power. Many feel the gains of the 1990s can be linked to the 1993 march, when nearly one million fags, dykes, and others were so empowered that they went back home thinking they could do anything. And they did.

28

Gertrude Stein

Gertrude Stein was an avant-garde writer and self-styled genius, whose Paris home became a salon for the leading artists and writers of the period between World Wars I and II. Pablo Picasso, Henri Matisse, Georges Braque, Sherwood Anderson, Ernest Hemingway—all were drawn by her eccentric literary reputation. One remark from Gertrude Stein could make or destroy careers and reputations.

In her own work, she attempted in writing to parallel the theories of Cubism. Her *Tender Buttons* (1914) brings the ideas of fragmentation and abstraction to the printed page, using words for visual and sound effect, not for any narrative cognizance. ("A rose is a rose is a rose.") Not all of her work was so abstract: *Three Lives* (1909) tells the stories of three working-class women, and it has been judged a minor masterpiece by some critics. Her best-known book is *The Autobiography of Alice B. Toklas* (1933), actually Stein's own autobiography, from which her insightful observations on life and culture influenced a generation.

There were also the theater pieces, greatly inspiring the intelligensia.

The performance in the United States of her *Four Saints in Three Acts* (1934)—which the (gay) composer Virgil Thomson had made into an opera—led to a phenomenally successful American lecture tour in 1934–1935. At her side was her lifelong partner, Alice B. Toklas, whose all-consuming loyalty to Stein, as well as her steady encouragement of the artists who gathered in her home, makes her as much a reason for pride. In their lives and in their art, Stein and Toklas left gigantic imprints on the twentieth century.

29

Pre-War Berlin

Move over, Greenwich Village. The world's first self-aware, undisguised, gay urban experience existed in pre-war Berlin. Much has been celebrated about the social, cultural, and artistic achievements of the German capital before Hitler came to power. Music, theater, film, literature—Berlin led the world in all of that, and much of the energy and creativity of the movement was fueled by the rich gay subculture that thrived in the 1920s and early '30s. During that time, more than one hundred gay gathering spaces existed in Berlin; "lesbian chic" was fashionable decades before Madison Avenue coined the term; and Dr. Magnus Hirschfeld, the founder of Berlin's Institute for Sexual Science, challenged academia with his pioneering—and affirming—studies of same-sex relationships.

The liberal environment in Berlin encouraged pride, not shame, in one's sexuality. Gay, lesbian, and even transsexual publications abounded. People gathered openly; Marlene Dietrich came out of this culture, forever shaped by the openness and affirmation of pre-war

Berlin. The city led the way in the understanding of homosexuality as a naturally occurring part of the human condition. Hirschfeld's Institute was the first—and until after World War II, the last—attempt at the academic institutionalization of sexual science. Such a climate shaped the works of such diverse artists, gay and straight, as Oskar Kokoschka, Christoher Isherwood, Kurt Gerron, Max Beckmann, Käthe Kollwitz, Fritz Lang, Max Reinhardt, Carl Mayer, Ernst Lubitsch, and F. W. Murnau—as well as many others.

But the liberal climate of the 1920s found a sudden end with the coming to power of Hitler in 1933. Artists were seen as "degenerates," gay men as "state enemies." The Nazis shut down all the gay and lesbian spaces in early 1933, cutting off the lifeblood of the city. Two months later the Nazis dissolved the Institute for Sexual Science and burned the books from Hirschfeld's library on the Berlin Bebel square. Pre-war Berlin would only be a memory, evoked in Isherwood's *Berlin Stories*—which became *Cabaret*. Only sixty years later, with the fall of the Wall, did Berlin find the opportunity to reclaim its glorious past.

30

The Sexual Revolution

The "Swinging Sixties"? Thank the gay boys with their long hair and flower-patched jeans and the dykes who defied gender roles every time they straddled a Harley. In the 1960s, the rules were rewritten for sexual and gender behavior. Much of that is owed to the political mobilization of the gay movement, which destabilized the rigid boundary between social obligation and individual expression. Okay, so we can lament the excesses of the sexual revolution: an increase in unwanted pregnancies, sexually transmitted diseases, AIDS. But the real legacy of the era was a new, open-minded attitude toward sex. We forget now, here in the jaded twenty-first century, just how repressed a world it once was, how Lucy and Ricky slept in separate beds and no one questioned how Little Ricky was born, how girls got married without really knowing what to expect, how shameful it was to talk about things that now seem tame. Shame ruled in those days. So many mistruths. So much fear.

But for the generation growing up in the 1960s, a radically different attitude toward sex developed. Communal living situations fostered sexual experimentation. Groups like the Sexual Freedom League advertised orgies and "love-ins." In parks, at festivals, at almost every hippie gathering there was the occasion for newly formed "couples" to make love, often in public view. "Free love" meant just what it said: love anyone, anywhere, anytime, without guilt. Certainly the visibility of gays and lesbians standing up for who they were helped push the sexual revolution toward its goals.

While much of the bacchanalia now seems dated, even quaint, the lessons have been taken to heart. Knowledge is a good thing; shame is unnecessary. Women were allowed, for the first time since ancient days, to define their sexuality on their terms. And while the excesses of the revolution left their mark, no one can deny the true legacy of the era: sexuality was validated as an important, vital part of human nature, and no one need ever feel ashamed or alone.

31

West Hollywood

You gotta love WeHo. Its origin was not unlike Mickey and Judy putting on a show. A bunch of gay folks decide to make a city of their own and, as improbably as those old Mickey-and-Judy extravaganzas, it works. Spectacularly.

Gays and lesbians have always lived in West Hollywood, coexisting with bohemian straight populations drawn to the edgy nightlife along the Sunset Strip. In the 1960s, young people from all over the nation flocked to such West Hollywood clubs as the Whiskey A-Go-Go and the Troubadour. WeHo became the center of a thriving music industry. And, as an unincorporated section of Los Angeles County, it was beyond the reach of the homophobic Los Angeles Police Department. No wonder the gay influx skyrocketed by the 1970s.

In 1983 a grassroots movement to incorporate West Hollywood into its own, autonomous city took hold. Residents, many of them gay, mobilized to put the issue to a vote in the November 1984 election, and the proposal passed handily. From the start there was a large gay presence in city government. A few years later, when the Los Angeles County Sheriff's Department fired a gay deputy, gay political pressure ended the city's contract with the Sheriff's Department in favor of a police force that might better reflect the population of 36,000, which was estimated at that point to be one-third gay. Although voters narrowly decided to keep the Sheriff's Department, the close brush with losing the lucrative contract with WeHo prompted the department to improve its relationship with gay residents. Today, residents and city officials report, several openly gay deputies serve in the station.

West Hollywood proved the political power of gay communities. It's also given the rest of the nation a city that is often cited as a model. It is a city that actively encourages the arts, supports rent control, empowers elderly activists, and promotes tolerance. A city gun-control ordinance served as a blueprint for a similar statewide law. Its "resident revolution" has been seen as evidence that communities really can take control of their lives. And while the city still struggles with crime, traffic, and noise pollution, it's still a brilliant, successful example of a progressive government at work.

32

Outweek

Sometimes you just need a good kick in the ass. That's what *Outweek* did for a generation of gay activists—indeed, for the gay and lesbian movement, still shell-shocked in the late 1980s by the twin blows of AIDS and Ronald Reagan. Inspired by the direct-action, in-your-face politics of ACT UP, *Outweek* was a magazine founded in 1989 in New York by, among others, Kendall Morrison, to finally give America's premier city a gay publication of its own. No one expected the furor it would cause.

Today when you mention *Outweek* most people think "outing," as if that's all the magazine did. True, it did pretty much set the standard in dragging people out of the closet, infuriating both heterosexuals and moderate homos. It's fascinating today to see how its philosophy has gone mainstream, with even Barbara Walters on national TV pressing Ricky Martin about whether or not he's gay. No one thinks it's inappropriate anymore; it's a valid journalistic inquiry. But when *Outweek*—especially in Michelangelo Signorile's column, in which he used lots of

CAPITAL LETTERS—pushed the same issue with Malcolm Forbes, or Richard Chamberlain, or Liz Smith, or Chastity Bono, the magazine was called radical, self-defeating, destructive. How times change.

But *Outweek* was never just about outing. Articles challenged gays to reconsider long-held opinions and biases. Sexism, racism, transphobia, sexphobia—all were named. No one was safe. Not closeted gays. Not straight allies (remember the "I Hate Straights" issue?). Not any one of us. *Outweek* produced a new spin on what was *really* going on during the first Bush presidency; the absence of such a voice under Bush II has been very keenly felt.

The journalistic techniques of *Outweek,* no matter how abrasive, changed the media. Editor Gabriel Rotello insisted they were simply trying to equalize "the way gay and straight people were treated by reporters," and in doing so, they helped erase much of the demonization and marginalization of gay lives. *Outweek* pushed the gay movement toward demanding change, instead of simply asking politely and being content with crumbs. The stunning integration that we've witnessed over the past few years, with gay lives and gay stories and gay faces so much a part of American media, is owed in large degree to the daring, defiant politics first expressed in the pages of *Outweek.*

33

Queer Studies

In the 1990s a new academic movement spread across North American campuses. "Queer studies" it was called—and it helped change academia. It allowed academics to reconsider (always a good thing, reconsidering) old ways of looking at society, culture, history, art. Queer theory offered the radical idea that things like gender or sexuality are socially constructed, and so are mutable and shifting. This way of thinking opened up a whole new way of considering anything that had appeared in the past to be eternal, essential, or unshakably true. Perhaps, instead, such things could be better understood through challenge rather than unquestioned acceptance. Such is, after all, the soul of intellectual pursuit—an academic truth of which queer theorists reminded the rest of academia.

Indeed, queer studies has been credited with reinvigorating debate on campuses. Just think of what the word *queer* implies: odd, peculiar, out of the ordinary. Queer study concerns itself with expressions of sexuality that are "queer" in this sense, and by extension, with the behaviors and identities that arise from it. Following feminist theory, queer theory examines the complex array of social codes and forces that interact to shape the ideas of what is normative and what is deviant at any particular moment. Such reconsideration of the essential—and "God-given"—brought about some of the liveliest academic debate seen in decades.

On a practical level, too, queer studies has established a place on campus for the examination of the roles that gays and lesbians have played in history. Today students, gay and straight, are taught the achievements and impact made by movements and people who have fallen outside the traditional model.

34

Andy Warhol

Soup cans? Celebrity? Wild hair? Andy Warhol's "American Pop" became perhaps the most influential trend in the art world in the latter half of the twentieth century. He introduced the concept of life itself being considered an art. He focused not so much on the end result, but rather on the creative process that he went through in order to produce his art: hence, movies that go on without any apparent action, silk screens that were handmade, performance art that is fluid and never the same thing twice.

Warhol's peak years were between 1962 and 1968, with most of his creativity happening within the confines of his New York studio, which he called "the Factory." The name was his play on the relationship between art and consumerism. His output at the Factory ranged from portraits of celebrities, car crashes, and a wide array of consumer products—most famously, of course, those endless cans of Campbell's soup.

Andy was also making movies, initially just experimental little snippets of life. Between 1963 and 1966, he made nearly fifty short films with titles such as *Sleep, Kiss, Haircut, Eat, Blow Job,* and *Taylor Mead's Ass.* Awarded the Independent Film Award by Film Culture, this series of quirky, self-conscious films proved Warhol's point that anybody could take subjects and film them—and even, especially if the viewer had smoked a little weed ahead of time, make them interesting. From this came Andy's oft-repeated quote: "In the future, everybody will be world-famous for fifteen minutes." Offbeat and eccentric, yes, but Andy Warhol was also uncannily prophetic.

His later films were more ambitious works: *Chelsea Girls, Lonesome Cowboys, Blue Movie.* But by now, Warhol's life—a menagerie of psychedelic parties peopled by counterculture types who defied traditional gender and sexual norms—was what made him most famous. His impact was enormous, shaking up our old notions of art and identity. By offering a space where unconventional artists could thrive, Warhol became one of the most important figures in the development of modern art in America.

35

Palm Springs

Not so long ago, Palm Springs wasn't much more than a few tacky motels and a couple of T-shirt shops with neon cacti out front. Today, it's become some of the most desirable real estate in the country—thanks to the makeover given this former Hollywood hotspot by its burgeoning gay population.

Observers credit Palm Springs' revitalization—with its art galleries, bistros, nightspots, restaurants, museums, acclaimed film festival, and popularity among tourists—to the influx of new residents during the mid-1990s. Today, more than 30 percent of the city's 48,000 year-round population is gay, and it's largely been gay money, gay ideas, and gay passion for the area that have once again made the playground of Frank Sinatra and the Rat Pack a tourist mecca.

It's a city (the metropolitan Coachella Valley numbers more than one million) that enjoys a small-town feel side-by-side with a cosmopolitan urban atmosphere. Different cultures have learned to coexist, from Mexican Americans to Native Americans to transplanted gays and lesbians, complementing each other and working together. Last year, an openly gay, African American man, Ron Oden, made history when he was elected mayor of Palm Springs. Additionally, openly gay Steve Pougnet was elected to the city council. The governing body of Palm Springs consists of five people: the mayor and the four city council-members. Three of those city leaders are now gay or lesbian.

"This is a warmly inclusive place," local philanthropist Harold Matzner told the magazine *Palm Springs Life.* "Not only forward-thinking, but forward-feeling." As the diverse crowd saunters down Palm Springs' revitalized main drag, his words could not be more true.

36

The Harlem Renaissance

The Harlem Renaissance, one of the most important cultural movements in American history, was one of the first flowerings of African American artistic achievement to be given recognition by the mainstream culture. And not surprisingly, a significant number of the movement's figures were gay or lesbian—or, in an effort for greater historical accuracy and inclusion, "non-heterosexual": Bessie Smith, Gladys Bentley, Ma Rainey, Countee Cullen, "Moms" Mabley, Alain Locke, Jessie Fauset, Zora Neale Hurston, Angelina Grimké, Claude McKay, Wallace Thurman, Richard Bruce Nugent, Mabel Hampton, Langston Hughes, and on and on.

It was a period of unparalleled artistic achievement. And, as is usually the case in such periods of artistic expression, there was a tolerance of all kinds of diversity. In Harlem during this period, many African Americans tolerated—even celebrated—homosexuality. Drag balls, commonplace during the period, were frequented often by the Harlem bohemians and intellectuals who wrote candidly about them in their correspondence. In speakeasies and buffet flats, gay sexuality was allowed generous expression. All of this contributed, as it did in pre-war Berlin, to the flowering of cultural and literary achievement.

The Harlem Renaissance left a lasting impact on nearly every artistic discipline: from poetry, memoir, and playwriting, to jazz, rock, and rhythm-and-blues. At a time when New York still had laws banning homosexuality and when gay bars were regularly raided and gay expression routinely squashed, it is remarkable that the Harlem Renaissance was propelled in so many ways by gay men and women.

37

Bertrand Delanoe

When he was elected mayor of Paris in 2001, Delanoe became the first openly gay person elected to lead a world-class city. (True, Berlin had had an openly gay interim mayor, Klaus Wowereit, but he had been appointed by city leaders.) Until then, Delanoe had been a little-known French politician from the Socialist Party. He'd never held a citywide office. Still, his election came after only two rounds of voting, helped by an alliance with the city's Green Party. Delanoe's election was hailed as a major political revolution against the right-wing forces that had controlled the City of Lights for the past century.

During his campaign, Delanoe didn't make sexual orientation a big issue, sticking instead to the idea that all politics are local: he campaigned largely on a platform of increased green spaces in the city and a reduction in the number of cars. True to his word, he created walkways along the Seine, and has, in general, rejuvenated the city's rich cultural vitality.

Delanoe's election proved that gay people are as electable to major public office as anyone else, smashing down barriers for those who might follow, particularly in less urban, less tolerant areas. And while he has never seen himself as a gay activist—so few of the true groundbreakers ever really see themselves that way—Delanoe nonetheless recognizes the special responsibilities and opportunities that have been given to him. He has championed the rights of same-sex couples and is an active member of antiracist groups. He has a future in leadership: Bertrand Delanoe is a politician to watch.

38

Marlene Dietrich

Marlene Dietrich was one of the few movie stars who ever told the truth. In repressive 1930s Hollywood, she lived with lovers both male and female, and by her very personality—honest and exotic—she redefined beauty and glamour. She stood for truth, for freedom (she was a staunch opponent of Fascism in her native Germany), and for sexual authenticity.

Observing that the best songs were written for men, Dietrich didn't complain: she just changed her clothes. Cross-dressing was part of her mystique. Her androgynous style appealed to men and women, gay and straight. Coming from Berlin, where sexuality was fluid and celebrated, Marlene conducted her lesbian affairs in Hollywood quite openly, crossing the confines of gender as no other star before her. Her greatest stage success had, in fact, been an obvious lesbian duet with Margo Lion in the revue *Es liegt in der Luft (It's in the Air)*. Two years later, in her American debut film *Morocco*, she walked out in a tuxedo, kissed a woman, and made Gary Cooper subservient to her. This androgyny guaranteed her success. Studio execs, usually so nervous about sexual transgression, let her do what she wanted: they understood a certain androgyny was part of the Dietrich image.

On top of her personal integrity, Dietrich left even more reasons to be proud. Right up to the front lines she'd go in her support of Allied troops in their fight against Hitler. With her seductive voice, she sang American love songs in her native German in order to seduce those Nazi soldiers listening to her on the underground radio. By standing against Fascism, by speaking out against the racism and fundamentalism that Hitler had inspired in her beloved Germany, Marlene was simply being consistent with her life values. The Nazis called her a traitor. In the light of history, she was a patriot of the highest order—a lesson to keep in mind today.

39

Andrew Harvey

The Eastern spiritual traditions—Hinduism and Buddhism especially—are supposedly more enlightened than Western Judeo-Christianity. But at times they still need a good shaking up, and one man, Andrew Harvey, did just that when his guru told him to dump his boyfriend and claim she'd "cured" him of his gayness. (And you thought only the American fundies were into conversion therapy!) Harvey, of English parentage, was born in India in 1952 and lived there until he was nine, a period he credits with shaping his Vision of the inner unity of all religions. At the age of twenty-one, he became the youngest person ever to be awarded the Fellow of All Souls College, England's highest academic honor. Returning to India to begin his spiritual search, he eventually became a devotee of the guru Mother Meera and began writing about Hindu philosophy in several books and articles. He was also the subject of the 1993 BBC documentary *The Making of a Mystic*.

That same year, however, Mother Meera ordered him to leave his partner and write a book about how her divine force turned him straight. Andrew Harvey disobeyed. He left his guru and took his lover as his husband. He was denounced, persecuted, and threatened with death by the supposedly peace-loving Hindu sect. But he also found enlightenment by incorporating Eastern mysticism with a Western vision of justice.

By breaking ties with the guru establishment in 1994, and devoting his writing to explaining the direct path to God, Andrew Harvey proved that no one spiritual tradition is the "right" one. He has taken the radical stand that sin and sex don't need to be reconciled, and that gay sexuality is innately spiritual. He has helped direct people, gay and straight, toward their own personal understanding and experience of God. Among his best-known titles are *The Tibetan Book of Living and Dying*, co-authored with Sogyal Rinpoche; *Dialogues with a Modern Mystic*; *The Essential Gay Mystics*; and *Son of Man*.

40

Cole Porter

Some of the most famous songs of the twentieth century were written by Cole Porter. "I Get a Kick Out of You." "I've Got You Under My Skin." "You're the Top." "Night and Day." "Too Darn Hot." "It's DeLovely." "Let's Do It" ("Let's Fall in Love"). Those who missed World War II might remember Porter best from the AIDS fund-raising album called *Red Hot and Blue,* in which contemporary pop stars put their own spin on Porter classics (Sinead O'Connor on "You Do Something to Me," Annie Lennox "Every Time We Say Goodbye," k.d. lang on "So in Love," Jimmy Sommerville on "From This Moment On," and lots more).

Many of Porter's most famous songs were originally presented in the context of musicals or movies. Some Cole Porter revues flopped on Broadway, but their songs lived on to become a part of the American musical fabric, being recorded by such popular singers as Louis Armstrong and Ella Fitzgerald. By the 1990s, in fact, ASCAP reported that the song "Night and Day" (originally from the musical *The Gay Divorcé*) had the highest sales numbers of all time.

Lots of Porter songs have little gay innuendos, and whole books have been written about how Porter's gayness—lived rather openly in Hollywood, with an understanding wife who looked the other way—influenced his musical compositions. But what makes Porter so timeless is his universal appeal, evidenced by how often his songs are still used as covers by new artists or in soundtracks to movies. His music is among the most engaging ever written in the history of pop standards—breezy, catchy, optimistic, filled with love and the spirit of life. How many of you, upon reading the titles of his songs above, immediately started singing a few bars to one of them? That's the mark of an enduring talent. Cole Porter—now, *he's* the top.

41

Drag

What would the world do without drag? It's the most obvious, most fundamental identity play we have. Put a wig on a guy and he adopts an entirely new personality. Add a dress and he's suddenly Ginger, or Roxie, or Bertha Venation, daring to do things he'd never do dressed as a man. Now, with the advent of drag kings, women can do the same kind of experimenting, slicking back their hair and sticking on a fake mustache to become Bruno, or Stanley, or Ben Dover.

Drag has traditionally educated and entertained us, from the Elizabethan actors who donned gowns to play Juliet to the drag queen balls captured in the film *Paris Is Burning*. Cross-dressing, by its very nature, calls into question rigid definitions of sex and gender that have the power to oppress, repress, and stifle creativity. It takes courage to do drag—exposing a side of one's self usually hidden from the world. Drag performers, like opera divas, perform with the kind of freedom that most people can enjoy only vicariously. Traditionally drag queens have been the toughest, fiercest, and most courageous figures in gay culture.

No wonder it was they who fought back at Stonewall and got the whole liberation thing rolling.

As the pop culture success of Boy George and RuPaul proved, mainstream audiences are fascinated by the spectacle of drag. While there will always be those for whom drag is only about who can look most like Bette Davis or Cher, the true legacy of drag is a brilliant tradition of satire. Indeed, some of the best and brightest satirists today are drag queens: Varla Jean Merman, the Kinsey Sicks, the Lady Bunny, Lypsinka, Coco Peru. The brilliant drag parodies of Charles Ludlam, Charles Busch, and Ryan Landry prove the adage: "Give a man a wig and you've given him a voice."

42

The Sony Building

Look up and feel the pride. With its Chippendale-style, broken-front-roof pediment, New York's AT&T Building—now the Sony Building—heralded a new era in architecture. Gay architect Philip Johnson's most famous public structure, built in 1984, stirred debate right from the beginning. To make this 197.5-meter-tall building look more monumental, Johnson topped it with its unique, curving, postmodernist Chippendale forms. Like Johnson's work on the Seagram Building for International Style, this building also proved a model and a new direction that others soon followed.

Design critics have observed that Johnson used the structure of a corporate office building as a piece of furniture, designed to fit into the "room" (city) around it. Johnson acknowledged Madison Avenue's identity as a shopping street by lifting the building twenty meters up from street level, with only its minimalist central lobby with its high arched bay on the actual street. A pioneer of modernism, Johnson revolutionized the relationship between architecture and daily life. He softened—even feminized—the forms of cultural institutions, making it acceptable to treat the high ideals of modernism as an aesthetic, using buildings for sensual, visual purposes. He left his mark on many of the famous buildings he designed, from the JFK Memorial in Dallas to the Lincoln and Kennedy Center theaters to the magnificent, gay-affirming Cathedral of Hope. But it is the Sony Building that many regard as his finest and most influential achievement. Despite a later remodeling of the street-level galleries, Johnson's imprint is still apparent.

But we miss the *Golden Boy* statue that Johnson rescued from the old AT&T Building and placed inside the new structure's lobby. Everyone going in or out of the building had to pass this charming male nude. The seven-meter Spirit of Communication by Evelyn B. Longman was removed to AT&T's New Jersey premises after Sony took over the Manhattan building. In January 2000, AT&T offered to return *Golden Boy* to New York, but in April they changed their minds and decided to keep it.

43

Bob Paris

By the time Bob Paris was twenty-three years old, he had won both the NPC National Championships and the IFBB World Championships (Mr. Universe), overcoming tremendous odds in doing so. He went from being a homeless teenager to a world champion—indeed, one of the most respected, celebrated, and photographed athletes in history. And along the way, he shattered many stereotypes about bodybuilding, masculinity, and homosexuality.

An artist as well as an athlete, Paris created a physique that went beyond the limitations and definitions of the competitive stage. Sculpting a classic physique while utilizing intelligent training techniques became his trademarks. Paris's books on fitness and health challenged the notion that bodybuilders were dim bulbs, while his announcement about being gay disproved the image of the weak, browbeaten homosexual.

So his much-publicized marriage to Rod Jackson went kaput. By being as honest and upfront as he is, Paris has become an inspiration on many levels. With his competitive career over, he did not retire into obscurity, but became an in-demand motivational speaker, lecturing on self-esteem issues and overcoming adversity. He has continued to write: his workout books—*Beyond Built, Flawless,* and *Natural Fitness*—are considered among the best in the field because they transcend the simple mechanics of exercise and diet, exploring the connection between fitness and self-esteem. He also penned an acclaimed personal memoir, *Gorilla Suit: My Adventures in Bodybuilding.* He has received thousands of letters from readers, gay and straight, who have taken hope from his words. Not only for his flawless physique does Bob Paris offer us reasons to be proud.

44

Tom of Finland

Perhaps no one has had a greater influence on gay male iconography than illustrator Tom of Finland. All those massively endowed men, with their square jaws and bubble butts, gave expression to the gay erotic psyche, so long denied representation. Born Touko Laaksonen on the southern Finnish coast in 1920, he was drawing from a very young age. A friend (to whom gay male culture will always be grateful) suggested he submit his charcoal illustrations to the American bodybuilding magazine *Physique Pictorial.* The magazine's spring 1957 issue featured a laughing lumberjack on its cover, drawn by "Tom of Finland." Tom's illustrations caused a sensation.

Tom always called his work his "dirty drawings," but in truth they are archetypes of fantasy. Most gay men have an immediate—and, er, visceral—reaction to seeing one of Tom's illustrations. True, he concentrated on muscular, hyper-masculine men, disdaining effeminate characteristics; yet his masculinity was always gay-affirming, even in his depictions of sado-masochistic scenes. His art was subversive in a repressive time: by day he toiled as an advertising exec, turning out his "dirty drawings" by night. Only by 1973 was he making enough money from his art to give up his day job.

Tom's numerous books guaranteed him a wide following. By the late 1970s he was also being taken seriously as an artist, having his work exhibited in museums and galleries worldwide. In 1984, with his friend Durk Dehner, he founded the Tom of Finland Foundation as a nonprofit educational archive to preserve, restore, and exhibit erotic art. When he died in 1991, Tom of Finland left behind a body of work (and what bodies they were!) that charted the course of much of gay male desire during the twentieth century.

45

Merchant-Ivory Films

A Room With a View, The Bostonians, The Europeans, Howards End, The Remains of the Day, Jefferson in Paris, Maurice—just one of those films would be reason enough to bust our buttons with pride, but the creative team of James Ivory, director, and Ismael Merchant, producer, has had an impressive track record of hits. They've been making films for the past twenty-five years, almost a film a year. They've been so successful that their conjoined names have become a Hollywood adjective, "very Merchant-Ivory," to describe a film of great literacy and visual beauty that deals with relationships between people—a rarity in this age of high-tech computer effects.

Partners in life as well as in work, Merchant and Ivory haven't had the success in recent years they enjoyed in the 1980s and 1990s (*Le Divorce* came and went with hardly anyone noticing). But in their moment they offered perhaps some of the finest character studies ever on film: Anthony Hopkins's insidious seduction of Emma Thompson in *Howards End*, the self-awakening of James Wilby in *Maurice* and of

Helena Bonham-Carter in *A Room With a View,* the secret yearnings of Vanessa Redgrave in *The Bostonians.* With often shoestring budgets and casts of less-than-box-office names, Merchant-Ivory turned out literate, bewitching films that endure long after the big summer extravaganzas have faded from memory.

What has made the Merchant-Ivory team so remarkable in the past is their ability to get films made that don't have "commercial blockbuster" written all over them. As the film industry shifts ever farther away from stories about people toward stories whose only purpose is to showcase special effects, the future for Merchant and Ivory seems to necessitate a return to their art-house roots. Let's just pray that, however they can manage it, they keep on making films.

46

The Violet Quill

There were influential gay writers before the Violet Quill group, of course, but this was an assembly of publicly identified, self-proclaiming gay men who were writing uncoded, gay-specific literature for the first time in history. Christopher Cox, Robert Ferro, Michael Grumley, Andrew Holleran, Felice Picano, Edmund White, and George Whitmore collectively represented the aspirations—and the achievements—of gay literature in the years immediately following Stonewall. Each author is reason enough for pride on his own, but together their work represents a generation's articulation of the values, principles, and prejudices of the culture of gay liberation. The work of the Violet Quill influenced not only succeeding gay writers, but all writers who dealt with issues of oppression, liberation, and the search for authenticity.

As a group, the seven met informally, sharing their work with each other, convinced only other openly gay writers could offer useful feedback. Although no formal charter was ever written for the Violet Quill, the members held common interests: a desire to reflect their gay experiences in specifically autobiographical fiction and a desire to write for gay readers first, ditching any attempt to have to "explain" or "justify" or otherwise ameliorate their lives for straight readers, without having to explain their point of view and language.

Just a quick perusal of some of the work that came out of the Violet Quill shows its tremendous appeal and influence. White has become internationally regarded as a great man of letters with such books as *A Boy's Own Story, Forgetting Elena,* and *The Beautiful Room Is Empty.* Holleran wrote the exquisite *Dancer from the Dance* and *Nights in Aruba.* Ferro came out with *The Family of Max Desir* and *Second Son*—the latter arguably the first novel about AIDS. Felice Picano has produced a diverse collection of thrillers and memoirs, as well as the blockbuster best-selling novel *Like People in History.*

The Violet Quill helped give voice to a generation, influencing generations to come, but just as important, showed the market that there was a demand for gay-themed literature. Every gay writer since owes an enormous debt to the Violet Quill.

47

Queer Cinema

The AIDS crisis produced a flurry of gay filmmaking in the United States, Canada, and Britain, while at the same time the independent film movement was gaining momentum. Together these two trends made possible one of the most influential cinematic movements in recent history, what's come to be called "queer cinema." In addition to giving us some brilliant, edgy films from a brash new perspective, the movement also gave some of today's leading filmmakers their start: Todd Haynes, Gus Van Sant, Christine Vachon, and many others.

Most of the first films in the queer cinema movement were underground or experimental in nature. Filmmakers like Sue Friedrich, Derek Jarman, Bill Sherwood (*Parting Glances*), and Donna Dietch (*Desert Hearts*) found success in art houses in major cities. Then, at the 1990 Sundance Film Festival, Jenny Livingston's *Paris Is Burning* and Todd Haynes' *Poison* won top honors, suddenly bringing queer cinema to mainstream attention. Gus Van Sant went from directing small gay-themed movies such as *Mala Noche* to mainstream hits like *Good Will*

Hunting—while still winning acclaim for his own smaller movies like *Gerry* and *Elephant*. Queer cinema redefined not only the independent film movement but also Hollywood cinema in general, by proving the artistic talents of its filmmakers and by showing that audiences of all kinds were hungry for offbeat characters and stories.

Today films like Haynes' *Far from Heaven* and Christine Vachon's *Boys Don't Cry* win top awards and pull in mainstream audiences. Once upon a time, gay activists complained about the homophobic traditions of Hollywood. Queer cinema changed how gay men and lesbians are portrayed on film, as well as how they might work behind the scenes. Even more than that, the influences of queer cinema have left a lasting impact on the artistic evolution of motion pictures.

48

Benjamin Britten

Benjamin Britten was one of the great composers and librettists of all time. His work brilliantly challenges the terms of critical response, questioning the relation among music, theatrical practice, and literature. Britten was one of the first to conceive gender and sexuality in terms of music—particularly opera—and its role in performances.

In the 1930s Britten wrote incidental music for plays and documentary films. He collaborated with W. H. Auden, whose poetry provided texts for the song cycles *Our Hunting Fathers* and *On This Island.* He was an accomplished pianist and often accompanied his lover, the tenor Peter Pears. In fact, Britten composed one of his greatest operas, *Peter Grimes,* for Pears, and with Pears and Eric Crozier, he founded the annual Aldeburgh Festival in 1948.

As is apparent in *Peter Grimes,* Britten was not afraid to deal with explicitly gay themes in his work. His opera *Death in Venice* closely follows Thomas Mann's story of a middle-aged man developing an all-consuming love for a teenage boy, and his *Billy Budd* retains all the homoeroticism of Melville's novel.

Britten's operas magnificently capture the heart and soul of the outsider. Though many critiques have appropriately contextualized his work with his life as a gay man, what makes Britten ultimately so transcendent is his appeal to all outsiders, to beautifully capturing the aching yearning to belong and to find love. Many consider him the greatest operatic composer of the twentieth century.

49

Sir Elton John

Reasons to love and admire Sir Elton? All one would need to do is list a few of his songs, which have become standards by which to judge great popular music. Take your pick: "Don't Let the Sun Go Down on Me." "Bennie and the Jets." "Your Song." "Goodbye Yellow Brick Road." "Funeral for a Friend." "Candle in the Wind"—at least before it was sapped up as a tribute to Princess Diana.

Born Reginald Kenneth Dwight in 1947 in Pinner, Middlesex, England, Elton started taking piano lessons at age four and won a scholarship to the Royal Academy of Music when he was eleven. In the early sixties he formed Bluesology, his first band. When he hooked up with lyricist Bernie Taupin, however, magic happened: between 1972 and 1975, Elton had seven consecutive number one albums, and he was selling out stadiums around the world.

There was a low point in his career, during which time he came out, then retracted the statement and got married, all the while he was putting out some less than spectacular albums. But by the early 1990s he was back on top, once again composing the songs that defined the latter half of the past century. He also became an AIDS activist, identifying himself with a cause that many celebrities were then afraid to touch. In 1992, he formed the Elton John AIDS Foundation, and since then all the profits from his singles are donated to this charity.

So a few more reasons, if any are even needed after all that: "Crocodile Rock," "Saturday Night's All Right," "I'm Still Standing," "Daniel." And where would we be without "The Bitch Is Back"?

50

The Gay Games

Lesbian long-distance runners? Gay wrestlers? Queer javelin tossers? Yep—you can find them all at the Gay Games, a series of athletic and cultural events, held every four years. Based on the principles of inclusion and participation, the Gay Games actually welcome everyone without regard to their sexual orientation. They also hold no minimum standards for qualification—so it really is a come-one, come-all experience. The only requirement is the desire to support the ideals of the Games, which is to reach for one's own personal best. They're also a great reason to throw one helluva boy-watching or girl-watching party.

Athletes who've participated in the Gay Games have come back with stories not only of personal achievement but also of the experience of solidarity felt with other participants. Originally called the "Gay Olympics" by founder Tom Waddell until the official Olympics committee threw a fit, the Gay Games dispel stereotypes while fostering and celebrating a sense of diverse community. Here's their officially stated raison d'être: "The purpose of the Federation of Gay Games is to foster the self-respect of lesbians and gay men throughout the world and to engender respect and understanding from the non-gay world, primarily through an organized international participatory athletic and cultural event held every four years." That alone is enough to swell our hearts with pride.

But here are a few other reasons as well: Mike Faraci and Kris Landher, medalists in wrestling; Diane Russel and Caroline Peck, rock climbing; Joseph Diaz, track and field; Jon Olsen and Gini Maulfair, swimming; the Miami Carnivores, volleyball; Tim Halverson and Jayne Moore, bowling; Paul Shepard, tennis; the San Diego Cygnets, water polo. The list could go on and on, but these everyday Joes and Janes are reasons for pride as much as any of the celebrities elsewhere in this book.

51

Queen

"We will, we will rock you." And they did, spectacularly. Queen was like no rock band, before or since, and it defined the music of a generation. Brian May, John Deacon, Roger Taylor, and Freddie Mercury—Queen was known for heavy metal, glam rock, and camp theatrics set against the sound of layered guitars and overdubbed vocals. How many tough young straight boys rocked out to the stirring vocals of Freddie Mercury—whose flamboyant sexuality was in fact what made Queen so unique.

The group was grounded in 1971 when May (guitar) and Taylor (drums) hooked up Freddie Mercury (vocals and piano). A few months later Deacon (bass) completed the band. Their first album, the eponymous *Queen*, was greeted with critical hostility, as were the group's early live performances—no doubt because of the implied queerness of its name and Mercury's effeminate, long-haired, heavily made-up stage persona. Yet they changed nothing, forging on ahead with *Queen II*—which was unexpectedly the huge breakout success of 1974.

Welcome to the era of glam rock, a genre quickly overtaken by a macho heterosexuality but, as its mascara and sequined origins suggest, was really an expression of gay culture. Queen ruled the charts in the late 1970s, with *Killer Queen* climbing to number two on the British charts. Their fourth album, *A Night at the Opera* (1975), was the most expensive rock record ever made at the time of its release, and its first single, "Bohemian Rhapsody," became one of the great rock anthems of all time. It was Queen's greatest hit and offered the world one of the first conceptual music videos.

Mercury became an icon for the generation growing up in the late 1970s and early '80s, inspiring both gay and straight teens with his style as much as his music. That he was able to maintain this status in spite of regular attacks from gay-baiting DJs is/was a singular achievement. In 1992, when Mercury died of AIDS, a huge memorial concert was held at Wembley Stadium, featuring such artists as Elton John, David Bowie, Liza Minnelli, and George Michael, testifying to the enduring legacy of Queen.

52

Paul Monette

Monette's was one of the great voices of our times. As a poet he produced two collections: *The Carpenter at the Asylum* (1975) and *No Witnesses* (1981). He then turned to writing novels, achieving acclaim in 1978 for *Taking Care of Mrs. Carroll.* But it wasn't until both he and his lover, Roger Horwitz, were diagnosed with HIV that Monette's voice suddenly became transcendent. In 1988 he wrote *On Borrowed Time,* a memoir of living with AIDS and of his lover's death. Its passion, anger, and terrifying beauty makes it perhaps the finest work written during the immediacy of the AIDS crisis. Almost single-handedly at the time, Monette succeeded in bringing AIDS to the forefront in contemporary literature.

During Roger's twenty-month illness, Monette had experimented with a form of poetry that would express his anxiety and sense of isolation. *Love Alone: 18 Elegies for Rog,* changed the face of AIDS in literature. Too often it had been about "someone else," as seen through the eyes of outsiders, observers, heterosexuals. Here it was compellingly personal, written from the heart.

Monette was constantly surprising critics who felt he had reached as far as he could go in his art. In 1992, he wrote what most consider his masterpiece: *Becoming a Man: Half a Life Story,* his National Book Award–winning autobiography. Monette wrote of the pain of being closeted, the effect it had on his writing, and how it shaped and hurt his life. It is no mere memoir; it is an evocation of struggle and salvation. Monette's writing is timeless and universal; it is not just about the struggle against the closet; it is more than just an account of life during the AIDS epidemic. Through his passion, through his cry to humanity for compassion, Monette gave voice to all people in struggle. Paul Monette died of AIDS in 1995.

53

West Side Story

"There's a place for us, somewhere a place for us." Next time you see a revival of *West Side Story,* or watch the film with Natalie Wood, or listen to the soundtrack, thank a gay man. Or rather, thank four gay men: composer Leonard Bernstein, lyricist Stephen Sondheim, librettist Arthur Laurents, and choreographer-director Jerome Robbins. At its heart, *West Side Story* is Romeo and Juliet—but it's also the story of any love denied, forbidden, or hidden away. That the musical has long resonated with gay audiences is not surprising—indeed, with what audience would it *not* resonate? Anyone who has ever loved, anyone whose heart has ever been broken, is moved by *West Side Story.*

Is it the most famous Broadway musical of all time? Certainly its songs have worked their way into our popular culture. Who can't sing a few bars of "I Feel Pretty"? At the time, the musical was a major departure for Broadway, transforming a genre known for fluff and puff into "serious art" making social commentary. *West Side Story* transgresses the social order, daring to make a case for those who are different and marginalized.

In his autobiography, Arthur Laurents would humbly insist that *West Side Story* was more influential in content than form, but he admitted: "What we did was take every musical theatre technique as far as it could be taken. Scene, song, and dance were integrated seamlessly; we did it all better than anyone ever had before. We were not the innovators we were called but what we did achieve was more than enough to be proud of."

54

Of Human Bondage

Somerset Maugham's greatest work, *Of Human Bondage* is a bold, disturbing novel that has left an enormous mark on the literature of human desire. First published in 1915, it's a veiled autobiography, with Maugham changing the gender of his protagonist's object of desire. The story concerns Philip Carey, a sensitive boy born with a club foot; in Maugham's own case, it was a bad stammer that made him feel freakish and alienated. Philip attempts to chart out a life as an artist, but becomes obsessed with a base, boorish waitress named Mildred. It's an obsession that nearly drives him mad. There is no more powerful story of sexual infatuation, of human longing for connection and freedom.

It was a viewpoint shared right from the start by readers and critics alike. "Here is a novel of the utmost importance," wrote Theodore Dreiser on publication. "It is a beacon of light by which the wanderer may be guided. One feels as though one were sitting before a splendid Shiraz of priceless texture and intricate weave, admiring, feeling, responding sensually to its colors and tones." Half a century later, Gore

Vidal had similar praise: "It is very difficult for a writer of my generation, if he is honest, to pretend indifference to the work of Somerset Maugham. He was always so entirely there."

The film version of *Of Human Bondage* left its mark as well, with the talent of Bette Davis as Mildred exploding onto the screen for the first time. It is one of the most haunting, powerful stories of English literature.

55

Noël Coward

We just don't seem to have Renaissance men anymore. Noël Coward—now there's an example of a true Renaissance man. Playwright, composer, actor, film producer, poet, singer, dancer, raconteur—Coward was legendary for his wit and satire. Just a few of the treasures he gave to the world: musical compositions like "Mad About the Boy," "Twentieth Century Blues," and "My Secret Heart"; plays like the brilliant bisexual ménage à trois *Design for Living,* the superbly ironic, innuendo-ridden *Private Lives,* and the poignant *A Song at Twilight;* witty on-stage repartee in sketches and parodies that paired him with the likes of Bea Lillie, Gertrude Lawrence, and Fred Astaire.

But for many his finest achievement was *Brief Encounter,* the film he produced based on his play *Still Life.* The heartbreaking story of a fateful encounter in a train station, in which a seemingly happy, content woman envisions a life beyond what she has settled for, stirs the wistful wanderlust in all of us, raising the most achingly lonely question of all: "What if?" The acting (Celia Johnson and Trevor Howard), direction

(David Lean), and score (Rachmaninov) are all superb, yet it is the vision of Noël Coward that brings it all to life.

Much of Coward's work is imbued with his own experience of a gay man; there's a whole literature now on the gay sensibility of Coward's plays and music. He was discreet but never inauthentic, even penning an unproduced play called *Volcano*, which included a gay relationship among its characters. It's a fascinating coda to a career that spanned seven decades and at least as many disciplines. Noël Coward was truly one of the irreplaceables.

56

Frida Kahlo

Today, decades after her death, artist Frida Kahlo has become an industry unto herself. Volvo uses her image to sell cars. The U.S. Postal Service put her face on a stamp, and she made the cover of *Time* magazine. A movie of her life brought star Salma Hayek an Academy-Award nomination. Not bad for a woman who was supposed to be the "secondary artist," the acolyte, to husband Diego Rivera.

Yet even during her lifetime, Kahlo was recognized for her uniqueness in combining surrealism with her own highly personal subject matter. Until the 1970s, however, the prevailing sexism of the art world only rarely elevated a woman to the status of "great." With the reconsiderations of the past few decades, Frida Kahlo is now one of the most influential artists of all time.

True, she possessed a great and often overriding love for Rivera, but her own gender play bespoke a deep passion for women as well. She often had affairs with Rivera's own mistresses, not to mention movie stars Dolores Del Rio, Paulette Goddard, and Maria Felix as well as photographer Tina Modotti and poet Pita Amor. She used cross-dressing—male drag—to project an aura of power and independence.

Eternally struggling with disabilities left from a youthful bus accident as well as Rivera's numerous emotional infidelities, Kahlo created art that depicts the depth of human misery. Yet while raw and often graphic, Kahlo's art always manages to portray her indomitable strength. After doctors revealed she would have to lose one of her legs, Kahlo drew a picture of two disembodied feet in her diary and wrote, ironically, that she'd now be one of the most instantly recognizable artists in the world. That she has become. An icon of personal pain and struggle but without a sense of victimhood, Frida Kahlo, and her art, are enduring symbols of strength and survival.

57

Oscar Wilde

Perhaps the greatest wit of all time, Oscar Wilde was also a man of extraordinary courage. Wilde's first and only novel, *The Picture of Dorian Gray,* was published in 1890. Its implied homoeroticism scandalized the Victorian guardians of morality and played a considerable part in Wilde's later legal problems. His subsequent work, all plays—*Lady Windemere's Fan, A Woman of No Importance, An Ideal Husband,* and *The Importance of Being Earnest*—all contained his trademark subversive tweak of popular customs and mores. They were also highly acclaimed and firmly established Wilde as one of the late nineteenth century's most notable playwrights.

Like generations of later gay men, Wilde's wit and flamboyance made him very popular in society. A sparkling dinner companion, endlessly quotable, he nonetheless made some people distinctly uncomfortable with how brazen he could be. When the father of his lover, Alfred Lord Douglas, accused Wilde of homosexuality, Wilde became the first famous gay man to be pilloried by the mass press. He was convicted of sodomy and sentenced to two years hard labor. His sons were taken from him, he was declared bankrupt, his house and belongings were auctioned off, and many of his friends deserted him.

Upon his release, Wilde wrote *The Ballad of Reading Gaol*, which recounted his harrowing experiences in prison. It is a brave, poignant, thoughtful, bittersweet narrative. Unfortunately, prison seems to have stifled his old wit and joie de vivre, and he wrote very little afterward. He spent the last three years of his life wandering Europe, staying with friends and living in cheap hotels. Oscar Wilde died in 1900.

58

James Baldwin

Baldwin was one of the most brilliant authors ever to consider the essentials of what constitutes identity. He also documented (and dissected) the American civil rights struggles in critical essays that challenge basic conceptions of American history. In addition, he wrote three plays, a children's storybook, and a book of short stories. James Baldwin was, in short, one of the great minds of the twentieth century.

He gained fame with his first novel, *Go Tell It on the Mountain,* a story of hidden sins, guilt, and religious torments. In this and other works, Baldwin combined autobiographical material with stirring analyses of social injustices. In *Another Country,* he dared to write about both racial and gay sexual tensions within the New York intellectual scene. His courage in including gay themes resulted not only in controversy from the white literary establishment but also brought him criticism from black communities. Being undisguised as a gay man, and as an African American gay man, required extraordinary courage and integrity. (Though he never embraced the label "gay," he always said he was "open to love" no matter the gender.)

Baldwin's second novel, *Giovanni's Room,* dealt explicitly with the theme of a man's struggle with his homosexuality. David, the narrator, tells his story on a single night. He is a young, bisexual American, and Giovanni is his Italian lover, who is to be executed as a murderer. It is truly one of the finest, most emotionally honest novels ever written.

Baldwin was ahead of his time, writing about the implication and intersection of race, gender, and sexuality. His work is universal, his lessons ever timely. *Love takes off masks that we fear we cannot live without,* he once wrote, *and know we cannot live within.* About freedom, he observed: *Freedom is not something that anybody can be given. Freedom is something people take, and people are as free as they want to be.* And this: *It's not the world that was my oppressor, because what the world does to you, if the world does it to you long enough and effectively enough, you begin to do to yourself.*

59

Barney Frank

I have a friend who, whenever he watches some puffed-up right-winger spewing a lot of hot air, shouts at the TV: "Sic Barney on him!" He's talking about Barney Frank—openly gay congressman from Massachusetts, with the sharpest tongue on the Hill and the courage of the gods. There's nobody Barney isn't afraid to stand up to. He's a refreshing politician, speaking his mind, calling things the way he sees them. To listen to Barney Frank on Sunday morning news programs is to enter a "no-spin" zone.

Frank was first elected to the U.S. House of Representatives in 1980 and was reelected to nine consecutive terms, representing the Fourth Congressional District of Massachusetts. He's also a graduate of Harvard Law School and a member of the Massachusetts Bar. He has published numerous articles on politics and public affairs, and in 1992 wrote the aptly titled *Speaking Frankly*, a look at the challenges facing American politics.

Barney Frank has never been afraid of challenge; he's never shrunk from a fight. When, before he was officially out, the right wing tried to make hay over the revelation of a gay relationship in the 1980s, he stood up to them and admitted he was gay, and he's been rewarded with landslide reelections ever since. He's clear in his criticism of the Republican party's unholy alliance with the religious right, speaking plainly that until that's severed, the fight for gay rights can never truly be bipartisan.

Frank for president? Unlikelier things have happened. But until that time, we can be glad we have Barney in the House and on our side. Go get them, Congressman!

60

Angels in America

It is, arguably, the greatest play of the past half century. "Play" doesn't even begin to describe it, however. Theatrical experience, literary epiphany—Tony Kushner's *Angels in America* is really two full-length plays: *Part I: Millennium Approaches* (winner of the 1993 Pulitzer Prize for drama) and *Part II: Perestroika* (winner of a Tony Award). These plays explore the sexual, racial, religious, political, and social issues that confronted the country during the Reagan years, as the AIDS epidemic first spread through the population.

Angels was one of the first plays to showcase, as real people, characters living with AIDS. Two of the main characters are infected: Prior, a decent, upstanding man who is selected by the angels to serve as prophet; and Roy Cohn, the hateful, self-loathing Communist witch-hunter and powerbroker who refuses his own diagnosis of AIDS.

What could have been a self-serving, obvious attempt at politically correct multi-culturalness instead is a transcendent piece of theater, rising above its crucial historical context to comment on eternal human truths. Other characters include Belize, an African American gay nurse, along with Hannah, a Mormon mother who comes to New York to try to untangle the mess of her closeted son and daughter-in-law's marriage. Jews, Christians, and agnostics; homosexuals and heterosexuals; blacks and whites; men and women; caregivers and patients; it is the soul of humanity about which Kushner actually writes.

While starting out as an off-Broadway play intended mainly for a gay audience, *Angels in America* moved to Broadway where it quickly became the hottest ticket in town. It was recently made into a superb HBO film directed by Mike Nichols and starring Al Pacino, Emma Thompson, Meryl Streep, and Mary Louise Parker. The film's success proved the play still has resonance, that its themes of humanity, redemption, guilt, accountability, and compassion continue to have relevance in our lives.

61

SAGE

No one's immune from growing old. And although the gay community lost a large segment of its population to AIDS, a large demographic of gay men and lesbians are now facing the eventuality of becoming senior citizens. What's life going to be like for people like me? Thankfully, SAGE—Senior Action in a Gay Environment—is paving the way.

For many years, older gay men and lesbians felt isolated and alone. Many had not come out until later in life; important community bonds had not been formed when they were younger. SAGE was established to ensure that professional assistance is available for gay seniors. Like all aging Americans, gay seniors face the onsetting problems of illness, reduced income, loss of friends and family, and increased isolation from society. The dual discrimination of ageism and homophobia often prevents gay seniors from seeking and finding the help they need to live happily and productively in their later years.

Through weekly home visits, SAGE's trained volunteers become the link to the outside world for many gay homebound and neighborhood-bound seniors. Volunteers and clients spend time talking, sharing hobbies, and establishing friendships. In many instances, these friendships become an important part of the life of the client as well as the volunteer. Though more and more gay and lesbian people are having children of their own, many do not have younger people in their lives to act as caregivers. SAGE offers that all-important cross-generational experience—in which both sides give as much as they take.

62

Rudy Galindo

Come on. Admit it. How many of you out there are addicted to figure skating? And how much of the reason is because hunky boys get to spin around in tight shiny spandex? And how many times have you said, "Oh, *that* one has *got* to be gay"? Yet surprisingly, very few figure skaters are out—but Rudy Galindo is, and he's proven a great sportsman on and off the ice.

Rudy was the first skater—and only man—to ever win two medals at the World Junior Championships (gold in singles and bronze in pairs in 1987). He's also won two U.S. National Championships in singles and three in pairs (with Kristi Yamaguchi), as well as placing third in two National Junior Men's Championships. He's also had six top three placements in the World Championships. In 1996, he won an Olympic bronze medal in the Men's event in a competition that people still remember as one of the best ever.

In 2000, Galindo also went public with his HIV status. Like Magic Johnson, he's shown that being HIV-positive does not hinder him from being a top-flight athlete. After his diagnosis, Rudy went back to work, rejoining the Champions on Ice Summer Tour and skating throughout. He serves as an honorary chairman of the National Minority AIDS Council and has promoted the organization's education campaign on HIV-related anemia.

Flashy, sassy, with an adorable smile, Rudy Galindo has proven a fantastic role model. In a sport that has suffered from glitz and hype (can you say "Tonya Harding"?) he has proven a figure of enormous integrity, talent, and courage.

63

The Laramie Project

Sometimes art can rise from the most horrific of events. After the brutal 1998 gay-bashing murder of college student Matthew Shepard in Laramie, Wyoming, a group of young actors and writers from a New York City theater company headed west to seek out Laramie residents—shopkeepers, teachers, students, bartenders, social workers—whose lives were affected by that terrible event. In the course of the riveting play that resulted from those conversations, the company members interview a cross-section of Laramie residents, who reveal as much about the collective psyche of their town as they do about the crime itself.

Among those whom we meet, and whose stories are interwoven throughout the narrative, are a University of Wyoming Theater Department teacher; a student who won a theater scholarship by performing (against his parents' wishes) a scene from *Angels in America;* a taxi driver who gave Matthew Shepard a ride; a teacher who was the first lesbian to be "outed" at Wyoming University; the bartender of the bar where Matthew was picked up; the cyclist who found an unconscious

Matthew; the officer who was first on the scene, and who later feared she had been exposed to the AIDS virus when it was determined that Matthew was HIV-positive. These stories are told alongside those of Matthew's killers, Aaron McKinney and Russell Henderson, whose friends recount their lives. The whole gut-wrenching experience climaxes with the impassioned courtroom speech from Dennis Shepard, Matthew's father, who asks that his son's killers be spared the death penalty.

What makes *The Laramie Project* so brilliant is that it does not simply rehash the tragic story for sensationalistic gain. Rather, it mines the lessons of Matthew's death, what it tells us about society. Over the course of the theater company's one-year stay in Laramie, the play explores how the Matthew Shepard incident exposed prejudice and fear in a town that denied the existence of either. It is a very human story of culpability, compassion, and courage—a model for the analysis of prejudice by examining its source.

64

Camille

Who can forget Garbo's dramatic deathbed scene, dying of tuberculosis but looking as if she simply had a mild case of the sniffles, radiantly backlit as she coughed delicately into a lace handkerchief? When Carol Burnett parodied the scene, hacking and snorting and wheezing as Harvey Korman (Robert Taylor) tried to embrace her, we saw the absurdity of it all. But what brilliant, beautiful absurdity it was.

Camille stands out in Hollywood annals as being a nearly all-gay production. It wasn't consciously planned that way, or even probably realized or articulated at the time. It was just one of those convergences that happened from time to time in the studios, given how many gays and lesbians were involved in crafting classic Hollywood. The film's director was the great George Cukor, one of the most noble gentlemen ever to make films, and a distinguished, undisguised gay man. It was written by Zoe Akins, a feisty gay woman who shared her home quite openly (at least during Hollywood's more liberal periods) with a female companion. It was produced by David Lewis, the lover of film director

James Whale. Its stars, of course, were Garbo, known for her earthy bisexuality, and Robert Taylor, who survivors recalled had an affair with the film's set decorator, Jack Moore. Costumes were done by Adrian, who despite a marriage to Janet Gaynor, everyone knew was gay, and when supporting players like Rex O'Malley and Rex Evans are thrown in, it becomes one of the gayest sets ever assembled on a studio backlot.

The film is stunning to watch, a prime example of expert moviemaking by craftspeople at their peak. Certainly Cukor's direction was rarely better, with the script honed perfectly and the performances all on key, top-notch. This is Garbo at her most exquisite and existential: only *Queen Christina* offers her as much an opportunity to convey such timeless sacrifice and regret. It is pure Hollywood magic, a treasure.

65

Larry Kramer

What would the world have done without Larry Kramer? Sure, he could come across as a scold, as a nag, as an angry ranter-and-raver. "So what?" he'd say. He said what needed to be said. Larry Kramer was the gay conscience during those terrible years of the late 1980s and 1990, and consciences don't play nice. Kramer held no sacred cows; everyone and everything were fair game for his scorn. Straight society and institutions were called on their homophobia and aggressive neglect of AIDS, but gay people were also often the targets of Larry's diatribes. Our internalized homophobia, our fear of direct action, our maddening, incapacitating allegiance to political correctness—all of these traits took blistering heat from Kramer. A generation of political activists were molded by Larry's absolute demand for honesty and action.

It helped that he also happened to be a great writer. From films— *Here We Go Round the Mulberry Bush* and *Women in Love*—to his hard-hitting play, *The Normal Heart,* one of the first ever to deal with AIDS, Kramer's words stirred audiences passionately. *The Normal Heart* went above and beyond most other writing about AIDS in that it empowered its protagonists and let the story unfold from their perspective. The play holds the record for the longest-running production at Joseph Papp's Public Theater in New York; at the Royal Court in London, it broke all existing box office records.

Indeed, Kramer's writings about the AIDS epidemic, collected in *Reports from the Holocaust: The Making of an AIDS Activist*, remind us why, in those harrowing early years, his voice was the one to mobilize ACT UP and other direct-action political responses. Kramer's last play, *The Destiny of Me,* was a runner-up for the Pulitzer Prize.

"We must love one another or die," Kramer said simply and profoundly during the height of the AIDS epidemic. Truer, more direct words have rarely ever been spoken.

66

Marcel Proust

Like I'm supposed to say something pithy and profound about Proust in three hundred words? Makes me think of the old Monty Python sketch: *Summarize Proust in fifteen seconds.* Okay, here goes: *Proust was a novelist. He was a philosopher. One of the world's greatest thinkers. Someone who profoundly influenced how we see ourselves and each other.*

Born in Paris, Marcel Proust spent most of his life in bed, confined to his apartment because he was a severe asthmatic with an extremely sensitive stomach and skin. His principal work is the mammoth, seven-volume novel *A la recherche du temps perdu,* which he began writing in 1907 and continued for the rest of his life (he died in 1922). Translated originally (and most famously) as *Remembrance of Things Past,* it's more accurate to refer to it in English as *In Search of Lost Time.*

Alexander Woollcott (another candidate for a 102nd spot on this list) once said, "Reading Proust is like bathing in someone else's dirty water." Certainly, spending that much time with one writer is an intimate exercise. With more than four hundred characters, stretching over forty years, *A la recherche du temps perdu* was sure to inspire a devoted cult for Proust. "Proust Said That" is a regular feature on the Internet—for in truth, with all those pages (more than three thousand!) Proust had something to say on just about anything you go looking for.

Yet there's no doubt that the work is one of the greatest achievements of Western imaginative literature. Proust was both a satirist and an analyst; his exploration of human sexuality, including in a major way homosexuality, was an affirming, enlightening leap into the future. He defied contemporary aesthetics (and still does) by saying that art is not in the artifacts: a beautiful painting or piece of sculpture—or indeed a great, literate novel—ultimately only has meaning if it can transfer something wise or affirming or spiritual to humankind.

Okay, that's more than fifteen seconds—but after all: Proust took fifteen *years* to get it all down!

67

The Dreamland Players

Who'd have thought that the work of a bunch of drugged-out dropouts from Baltimore, using a home-movie camera to shoot poorly lit flicks about psychos and dog turds, would prove to be so enduring?

John Waters was the kingpin of the group, a ragtag assortment of fags and freaks: David Lochary, Mink Stole, Edith Massey, and especially Divine, the three-hundred-pound drag queen who became his legendary star. Divine would appear in nine of Waters's movies: impersonating Jackie in a reenactment of the Kennedy assassination (*Eat Your Makeup*); being raped by a giant lobster (*Multiple Maniacs*); mooning over Tab Hunter (*Polyester*); rubbing fish all over her body while jumping on a trampoline (*Female Trouble*); and, most notoriously, eating dog turds (*Pink Flamingos*).

Everything Waters filmed was played on a broadly comic scale. His films have dialogue that is ridiculously melodramatic and performances that are absurdly overblown. His conceit is bad taste being elevated to a new aesthetic; one critic has said Waters' audiences had to laugh to keep from being repulsed. Like Warhol a decade earlier, being a Waters afficionado was a mark of hipness in the 1970s and '80s, a sign of being on the edge. Waters made possible a world in which rules and definitions exist only to be challenged, manipulated, ignored, and rewritten. Edie Massey's lament to David Lochary in *Female Trouble*—"Oh Gator, I'm so afraid you'll find a wife, have kids, get a job at an office. The world of the heterosexual is a sick and boring life"—has become a classic Waters moment of satirical social rebellion.

With *Polyester,* the Dreamland Players began an infiltration of the mainstream; but while Waters' films have become less anarchistic and designed for maximum "gross-out," they have retained his none-so-subtle twist of prevailing social and cultural norms, offering pointed commentary on class, race, and gender roles. *Hairspray,* both film and Broadway show (which alone would rate a mention here), is one of our great morality plays, written—with the kind of irony Waters has always prized—by a man long harangued for a supposed embrace of amorality. In their own twisted, subversive way, the films of John Waters and the Dreamland Players are among the most moral, and certainly the most honest, ever made.

68

Charles Demuth

Charles Demuth was one of the most influential masters of early-twentieth-century art. Praised by critics at the time for being one of the most creative American minds, Demuth created landmark architectural studies and extraordinary floral watercolors. He also painted the world-famous *The Figure 5 in Gold,* an anticipation of Pop Art and an influential icon of American modernism.

Demuth moved with ease through the worlds of international art. He socialized with the greatest writers and artists of his time, people like Andre Gide, Marsden Hartley, Gertrude Stein, Marcel Duchamp, and Eugene O'Neill. He spent much time in the art centers of the Northeast, Greenwich Village and Provincetown, where he associated with leftist writers and artists committed to both political and sexual liberation. Likely through this association, Demuth became one of the earliest artists to reveal his gay identity through forthright, positive depictions of homosexual desire.

Indeed, his major historical contribution may be how audaciously he confronted the scandalized reaction to his work *Distinguished Air* (1930), notable for its homoeroticism. When several exhibitions refused to show it, Demuth did not take it as a deterrence but rather as a challenge. He painted additional overtly homoerotic watercolors of sailors disrobing, fondling themselves, and even urinating alongside each other.

Yet as wonderful as these images are, Demuth's importance goes beyond them. Art historian Robert Hughes observed, "If these scenes of Greenwich Village bohemia were all that Demuth did, he would be remembered as a minor American esthete, somewhere between Aubrey Beardsley and Jules Pascin. But Demuth was an exceptional watercolorist and his still lifes and figure paintings, with their wiry contours and exquisite sense of color, the tones discreetly manipulated by blotting, are among the best things done in that medium by an American."

In the pantheon of the great American artists of all time, Charles Demuth rates very high indeed.

69

The Metropolitan Community Church

Who says gayness and Christianity don't mix? When in 1968 Troy Perry felt alone and rejected by the established Christian faiths, he founded a church that recognized the inherent dignity and worth of the gay individual. Today, the United Federation of Metropolitan Community Churches (better known as MCC) is the world's largest gay and lesbian spirituality organization. MCC became the first Christian denomination in history to proclaim the integration of spirituality and sexuality as part of its intrinsic mission.

The impact of MCC has come to extend far beyond its own membership, forging relationships and earning respect within the wider experience of Christianity. MCC has official observer status in the World Council of Churches. MCC leaders have served as evangelists for the healing of homophobia by spending many years in dialogue with church councils at the national, regional, and local levels across the world.

Since 1968, Metropolitan Community Churches have stood defiant in the face of adversity, offering safe havens for those rejected by other religious communities. They have become a vital part in the process of gay empowerment and identity building. On a practical level, it has often been MCC that has lent the space in local communities for various gay and lesbian organizations and projects. The church has been one of the leaders in the development of a globally connected gay community.

Despite all the complaints of proselytizing at the March on Washington in 2000, MCC in fact recognizes and celebrates the diversity of spiritual belief and practice, making it one of the few Christian churches to do so (the Unitarian-Universalist society is nondenominational). Within its own practice, MCC worship is a mixture of ritual, word, and song; no one denomination is allowed to dominate.

With more than three hundred churches all across the world, MCC has proven to be a place for community and advocacy as well as faith and spirit.

70

Gay Student Alliances

When I was a kid, I couldn't even imagine such a thing. How many gay people over the age of thirty would have given just about anything to have a school-sponsored space where gay and straight students could meet together in a safe, nonthreatening and honest way? Of course, it still would have taken quite the nerve to actually walk into one of those meetings—and it still does today. Which only affirms why such alliances are so important.

Various communities have their own systems, some better than others, while some schools still struggle through as if in the Dark Ages, leaving gay students to fend for themselves. Massachusetts might have a model Safe Schools Program, but many states have nothing at all. That's why groups like the Gay, Lesbian, Straight Education Network (GLSEN) have risen to fill in the gaps.

Here's their mission statement: "GLSEN envisions a world in which every child learns to respect and accept all people, regardless of sexual orientation or gender identity/ expression." The group combats the harassment and discrimination faced by students who don't quite fit the norm—both from other students *and* school personnel. When allowed to establish programs and work within the schools, GLSEN creates learning environments that affirm the inherent dignity of all students, and, in so doing, teaches them to respect and accept all of their classmates.

The key to ending anti-gay prejudice and hate-motivated violence has always been education. And while we have seen some amazing progress in urban and suburban areas, gay kids in more remote areas are often without support—which is why GLSEN has made outreach to the hinterlands a priority. Thousands of volunteers participate, working with local school boards, principals, educators, and school librarians to create positive change in hometown schools.

I think we can already see some of the impact from such work. Polls routinely show that young Americans by a much higher proportion have a positive view of gay and lesbian people; a majority of them favor gay marriage, for example. Those who work in the schools are doing the most important work there is. This is our future, and we can be thankful this is the generation who is set to inherit the culture.

71

The Daughters of Bilitis

Everything has to start somewhere. The beginning of every journey is a single step. All bromides aside, the Daughters of Bilitis took a stand when just about no one else would—not even the men of the fledgling "homophile" movement. The very first lesbian organization—founded in 1955 in San Francisco—the DOB recognized that the rights of gay women were not going to be won unless they themselves took up the fight. Accordingly, they began publishing a newsletter, *The Ladder*—the first attempt to connect the thousands of isolated women all across America.

The Ladder was a great success, with membership in the DOB growing so fast that by January 1957 the group's founders—among them, Phyllis Lyon and Del Martin—took out papers to become a legal, official, nonprofit organization of the State of California. The name of the organization came from the book *The Songs of Bilitis*, which contains love poems between women, and indeed, the rights of women were as important to the DOB as the rights of homosexuals. "How could we separate those two vital parts of our identity?" asked one early member.

Joining with the mostly male Mattachine Society, the DOB fought to reform the state's anti-homosexual laws. But the relationship with Mattachine and DOB became conflicted as the Women's Liberation Movement began to gain ground on the East Coast. Mattachine showed little interest in helping the women's movement, but meanwhile the Feminist Movement, led by Betty Friedan, wasn't exactly welcoming their support either. The National Organization for Women began to eject lesbians from its ranks, naming them "The Lavender Menace."

Although the DOB continued on for some years, this sad, unnecessary struggle—a collision of sexism and homophobia among two groups already oppressed by those some evils in the larger society—essentially spelled the end of the nation's first lesbian rights organization. Some women felt more drawn to the feminist cause, others to the gay cause; eventually the women's movement would embrace its lesbian members and the gay movement would work to become more inclusive. Much of that, in truth, is owed to the work of those original Daughters of Bilitis, who understood the path to true liberation is not through division but through unity.

72

The Ugly Duckling

Tell me this isn't a gay story. Tell me that we have not seen echoes of this simple, basic tale of humanity all throughout the ages, from Quasimodo and Ferdinand the Bull to Rudolph the Red-Nosed Reindeer and Herbie the Dentist Elf. Written by Hans Christian Andersen, a man who loved other men, *The Ugly Duckling* is an archetypal tale—as all the best fairy tales are—that proclaims the odd, the misfit, and the different are in fact possessors of a true and hidden beauty.

Most of Andersen's fairy tales contain humor that can be taken two ways, and it is this interaction between childish naïveté and adult irony that gives them such appeal. Many of them may be read as queer allegories, with some apparently autobiographical. *The Little Mermaid,* for example, was written after Andersen was heartbroken by the marriage of Edvard Collin, the love of his life. The love that could not be, between the mermaid and a human being, between two completely different species in a way, reflected Andersen's own experience. Other fairy tales have also endured—*Thumbelina, The Snow Queen, The Little Match*

Girl, The Will o' the Wisp, The Brave Tin Soldier, and many more—securing Andersen a place securely alongside the Brothers Grimm.

But it is *The Ugly Duckling* that stands as perhaps his most celebrated story, and the one that codifies most succinctly its universal truth. It is the story of the duckling who looked nothing like his brothers or sisters, who is taunted for his difference, his "ugliness." Even his mother rejects him. He endures a terrible winter of despair, and just as he is about to give it all up, he sees his reflection in the water: he has grown up to become a swan.

He had been persecuted and despised for his ugliness, and now he heard them say he was the most beautiful of all the birds, Andersen wrote. *I never dreamed of such happiness as this, the swan said, while I was an ugly duckling.*

Harvey Fierstein rewrote the story beautifully as *The Sissy Duckling,* bringing to the forefront the queer allusions in the tale. But the story's resonance is even more universal: it is a dream for all who are different.

73

Martina Navratilova

She was one of the greatest tennis players in history—indeed, many consider Martina Navratilova as the greatest female athlete of the twentieth century. Born in Prague, Czechoslovakia, in 1956, Navratilova found herself increasingly frustrated by the interferences of the Communist bureaucracy, which threatened to deny her exit visas because of her liberal viewpoints. In 1975, arriving to play in the U.S. Open, she defected to the United States, requesting political asylum. She became an American citizen in 1981.

As a Singles Tennis Player, Navratilova has won 167 titles. In 1984 she completed three quarters of a Slam, losing only in the last final, the Australian one: former compatriot Helena Sukova stopped Martina within a step from the Grand Slam. But she has scored a record nine wins at Wimbledon. Her victory in the 1995 Wimbledon Mixed Doubles extended her total Wimbledon titles to nineteen—one short of Billie Jean King's record (another candidate for that elusive 102nd slot).

What makes Navratilova even more of a hero is that, almost from the start, she was refreshingly honest about her sexuality. When the press commented on her relationship with the American writer Rita Mae Brown, Martina admitted to it and announced she was a lesbian. She was one of the first public figures ever to do so.

She is known for a steely determination and competitiveness, and that drive has secured her place in the pantheon of greats. When in the early 1990s the number One tennis crown had passed to the teenaged Monica Seles, thirty-seven-year-old Martina wasn't ready to go gracefully into retirement. On February 21, 1993, she achieved the greatest in her career: she defeated the number one Monica, taking three sets and a final tie-break.

In courage, in character, and in sheer athletic ability, Martina Navratilova is one of the all-time greats.

74

Women's Music Festivals

A cultural institution among lesbians for more than thirty years, women's music festivals are honored community events that have done much more than just provide a stage for talented musicians to regale the crowd. The festivals have become venues for empowerment and community building, and they celebrate women's space as much as their music. Every year throughout North America, dozens of festivals take place: the highly publicized, corporate-sponsored, mainstream Lilith Fair was indeed inspired by the long tradition of more regional women's music festivals. But these grassroots festivals truly offer the intimacy and sense of spirit that attendees have come to expect.

The first three women's music festivals—the National Women's Music Festival, which is still held annually at various sites; the Amazon Music Festival in Santa Cruz, California; and Womansphere in Maryland—took place in 1974. The best known of the festivals, however, was launched two years later: the legendary Michigan Womyn's Music Festival. Held during the second week of August, the Michigan festival has become the largest of all women's festivals, annually attracting more than 10,000 women to 650 acres of privately owned women's land in remote Hart, Michigan.

Like most of the festivals, the Michigan Womyn's Music Festival features more than just musical performances. Workshops, sporting events, nature walks, and support groups are held alongside myriad exhibits and services provided by female vendors. By keeping the event women-only, the Michigan festival tries to guarantee a safe space for women of all sexual orientations (with lesbians traditionally in the forefront of organization and promotion). Sadly, however, controversy has risen over the exclusion of transgendered women. Other festivals, such as the National Women's Music Festival, have become more inclusive, welcoming all, including men.

Regardless of the politics, however, the Women's Music Festivals have been an important cultural resource for thousands of women in building community and shaping their own identities.

75

The Radical Faeries

"The Faerie Circle," as the group is called within its ranks, is both political and spiritual in nature. It is a networking of "gentle men" devoted to the principles of ecology, spiritual truth, and a defining "gay-centeredness" in their identities.

Founded in 1979 by gay rights pioneer Harry Hay and his companion John Burnside, along with a small group of friends, the group chose the concept of "Faerie" in an attempt to reclaim a term long used to denigrate gay men. With the insertion of "radical" ahead of the "faerie," the group was committing to a radical break with social norms and conventions, advocating a "psychic return to the root of one's being."

The first "Spiritual Conference for Radical Faeries" was held in 1979, at the Sri Ram Ashram in Arizona, with more than two hundred men attending. The faeries based their practices on Wiccan and Native American rituals; like the faeries of legend, they would spend their gatherings dancing, feasting, and creating spectacle in a natural setting. Faerie ritual has become sacred to their members: the passing of a talisman from one speaker to another; ecstatic dance rituals, including the "Kali Fire," which banishes that which is no longer needed or desired; communal feasts; and often sensuous, erotic play.

What the Radical Faerie movement has done is remind gay men that a softer side—call it feminine—does not need to be rejected. The faeries revel in the sheer *difference* of being gay, in the absolute rejection of social and gender rules. While not every gay man is going to feel the need to hike into the woods, strap on a feathered headdress, and dance around a campfire, the faeries serve as a magical example of the inner beauty in all of us.

76

Melissa Etheridge

Her raw, edgy, heart-wrenching vocals and blues-based guitar riffs have led many to call Melissa Etheridge the Janis Joplin of the '90s. She has in fact proven to be one of the greatest rock musicians of all time.

Born in Leavenworth, Kansas, Etheridge was given her first guitar at the age of eight and wrote her first song by age ten. Studying at the Berklee College of Music in Boston, she dropped out after a year, moving to Los Angeles in 1982. It was a time when, as she's said, female singer-songwriters performing honest, straightforward songs with a bluesy rock flavor weren't exactly what the music industry was interested in. Still, she found a small but dedicated following—many of whom were, like herself, lesbian. Etheridge has given credit to her early gay supporters as giving her the momentum she needed for finally achieving her mainstream success.

In 1988, Etheridge's self-titled debut album was released and almost immediately went platinum. Her follow-up, *Brave and Crazy*, also went platinum, and in 1992 she won a Grammy for her track "Ain't It Heavy" from her album *Never Enough*. But it was her fourth album, *Yes I Am*, that skyrocketed her. It established her as one of rock's leading artists, with three top ten hits, one of which—the hauntingly beautiful "Come to My Window"—won her a second Grammy.

Yes I Am was a fitting title, as that same year Melissa, at an inauguration party for President Bill Clinton, announced that she was a lesbian. What her announcement revealed was that (like k.d. lang shortly before her) one could acknowledge one's gayness without necessarily having to endure a backlash to one's career. Etheridge's admission did not in any way alienate her wide base of fans; in fact, it seemed to galvanize them. As much as her music, Etheridge's complete authenticity is reason to celebrate her. She has become a vocal advocate for gay rights; her 1999 track "Scarecrow" was a tribute to gay-bashing victim Matthew Shepard.

77

Midnight Cowboy

In 1969, John Schlesinger made one of the greatest films of all time, one that is regularly included in Top Fifty or even Top Ten lists whenever they're assembled. This was *Midnight Cowboy,* adapted from the novel by James Leo Herlihy and starring Dustin Hoffman and Jon Voight. It was rated X—no film before had dared to show such a brutally honest account of the underbelly of New York City—but even so won Best Picture of the year. It is the story of Joe Buck, who comes to New York with dreams of making it big as a gigolo for rich women, but who instead finds connection with only one person, a soul as lost and lonely as himself: the tubercular Ratso Rizzo.

Through a series of vignettes, we see the bond grow between these two misfits: it's a twist on the old Hollywood love story—boy meets boy. Yet while Schlesinger would admit that *Midnight Cowboy* was about the love between two men, it can't be ghettoized as a gay love story. Joe and Ratso aren't homosexual: they're simply human, in the purest sense, and their love is about finding connection where we least expect it. In the end, what makes the film so lasting is its testament to human friendship, devotion, and love. "*Midnight Cowboy* is about the emergence of some sort of human dignity from degradation," Schlesinger once said, "and the need to feel for another human being."

Schlesinger, who was open about his gayness years before there was even a term for "coming out," also made the exquisitely beautiful *Sunday Bloody Sunday,* the first film to treat a gay relationship sympathetically and truthfully, as well as many other memorable movies. But *Midnight Cowboy* stands as his masterpiece and has become an American icon. The love story of Joe and Ratso is now considered one for the ages. In the final fadeout, after Ratso has died, Joe places his arm around his dead friend. It's an image etched into our souls: a symbol of the transforming power of love.

78

The Berdache

Not all cultures have oppressed their different children, and the Berdache stands as a symbol of the transforming power gayness can have when it is revered instead of persecuted.

In some Native American traditions, male children who exhibit at an early age what are perceived as feminine characteristics are valued by the tribe as a sacred trust. It is believed that the Great Spirit has sent this child as a liaison between males and females, a kind of translator or interpreter for the sexes. The "Berdache" is believed to have great wisdom into both sides of the human condition.

"Berdache" itself is a European term; the various Native American cultures all used different words to describe these gifts of Spirit (among the Zuni, for example, they are known as "lhamana"). The tradition itself was widespread, however, throughout the native peoples. Male Berdaches have been documented in more than 155 tribes. There was also a tradition of females whose proclivity for male lifestyles was also acknowledged, with such women becoming hunters, warriors, and even chiefs.

But it was the male Berdache who was more prevalent and afforded greater esteem. Such a child was apprenticed to a shaman, or the tribe's holy man. In the Berdache's training, he was taught (and in some cases, is still taught) the traditional work of both sexes. He dressed more like a woman than a man, however, and acted as a healer, a teacher, and often an arbiter for his people.

The concept of male and female spirits coexisting in one body was revered in native traditions, and the wise, proud Berdache offers great reason for pride. In his shamanic, reverential position, he represents a small corner of the world where people have been held in esteem for their differences rather than hunted down or exiled.

79

Archivists

As a historian, I am constantly grateful for the diligent, passionate work of archivists. Whether it be eighteenth-century household artifacts—ceramic plates, pewter cups, fragile fabrics—or Hollywood ephemera—letters from Hedda Hopper, photographs of nickelodeons, crumbling issues of *Photoplay*—these men and women preserve for all time fragments of our past, and they do so with deliberate care and love.

What's always surprised me is how often these people are gay. Wondering about it, posing the question to friends, I was offered several explanations for the phenomenon. Denied our own history for so long, many gay people have become passionate about preserving a record of the past. Not just the gay past—though there's a special sparkle in the eye when I ask them for something queer-specific—but all of the past, in all of its goodness, badness, beauty, and ugliness. Another reason may be that we may learn early how fleeting the moment is, how easily things are forgotten, and so we live with a greater desire to hold on to what is precious, what is tossed aside by the larger culture. And maybe we have a greater affinity for understanding the connection between then and now, between the past and the future.

Whatever the reason, I am very happy to report that—not to slight all the many wonderful straight archivists and librarians out there—our historical treasures are guarded by a large number of gay and lesbian hands. You might expect to find them at movie archives, carefully preserving the early-twentieth-century nitrate stock of the Vitagraph studios, for example, or the extravagantly beautiful lobby cards of the 1930s. But I have also found gay people in remote libraries, thoughtfully cataloging old city directories and ship passenger lists, which record the names of our ancestors' arrivals into this country. Gay curators in art museums, lesbian archivists in photography galleries—we have ensured that the past will still exist for future generations to study and learn from.

80

William Haines

He was the top male box office star in 1930, as popular then as Tom Cruise is today. The biography I wrote (*Wisecracker*) and a wonderful documentary by Randy Barbato and Fenton Bailey have brought him some renewed fame, but William Haines is still one of history's forgotten stars. And why? Because he dared stand up for who he was—and for the love of his life.

Born in Virginia, Haines entered films in the early 1920s. By 1926, with the twin hits *Brown of Harvard* and *Tell It to the Marines*, he had become a star. A Billy Haines picture was pretty formulaic: he's the arrogant jock who thinks he's God's gift—then has to eat "humble pie" before winning the girl. His was a new kind of screen personality, a kind of anti-hero decades before it was fashionable. Directors often played with his fey mannerisms: he's more in love with Jack Pickford than Mary Brian in *Brown of Harvard*, and *Way Out West* is one of the gayest films ever made.

By 1930, when he was at the top of the box office, having made a terrific transition to talking pictures, Billy Haines was well known as a wisecracking bachelor. But that bachelorhood was starting to cause snickerings in the gossip columns, prompting an ultimatum from MGM head honcho Louis B. Mayer: Billy was told to either give up his boyfriend (Jimmie Shields) and marry some starlet—or his contract wouldn't be renewed.

Of course, Billy was getting a little too old to play the cocky juvenile forever, but his unwillingness to play the studio game prevented him from being given a chance as a second lead or character player. When he told Mayer, in essence, where to put his ultimatum, William Haines was shown the door.

He was one of the few gay stars ever to refuse the "arranged marriage" or "photo-op" date. But still, he had the last laugh. Becoming an interior designer, Haines became legendary for his unique creations, which are still coveted today. He and Jimmie Shields were together for nearly fifty years. Billy Haines died in 1973.

81

Travel and Hospitality

Wherever you go, there we are. A friend once said to me he felt sorry for heterosexual tourists: they venture into some new city or foreign country totally on their own. Gay and lesbian travelers, on the other hand, armed with Spartacus or Damron guides, can immediately connect with people who welcome them like friends.

The travel and hospitality industries have been immeasurably shaped by their gay members. Like we can't credit a beautiful hotel room somewhere along the line to a fussy, demanding queen? Like we all haven't been relieved to see a gay man behind the counter at a reservation counter, knowing he'll make everything okay? Admit it: when you get on an airplane, you always scan the flight attendants to see if any are male (which, nine times out of ten, means gay) and hope you'll be in his section. Gay flight attendants have made many a long flight infinitely more enjoyable for me.

That's not to say that gay employees in the travel and hospitality industries give preferential treatment to their queer brothers and sisters.

Or maybe it *is* to say that. Whatever, I know I always feel better when I run into one of the family.

And that's not difficult: at Walt Disney World last fall, every other "cast member" was a cute boy allowing us to step ahead in line. Gay travel agents seem to know more than their straight counterparts when I'm planning a trip, advising on everything from car rentals to the best restaurants. Now we've got whole gay cruises, from RSVP to Atlantis to the all-women Olivia.

A friend of mine who's a hotel manager told me that, after a long career in hospitality, he really believes that it's been the gay employees who have set the standard for the industry. With all the traveling I do, I believe him.

82

The Yellow Brick Road

There are musings about the sexuality of its ultimate creator, novelist L. Frank Baum, but the Yellow Brick Road I'm talking about is the one from the movie, 1939's classic *The Wizard of Oz*. It's become an icon of popular culture—even Elton John used it as part of a song, and on an album cover, instantly conveying a sense of wonder and innocence and discovery. It's an image most of us can close our eyes and immediately conjure: those gleaming yellow bricks, stretching out through cornfields and poppies, continuing into infinity—thanks to the magic of painted backdrops.

The design and execution of the Yellow Brick Road was the work of gay hands. The MGM prop department was presided over by a group of remarkable men, all gay, from the chief, Edwin Willis, through the talented decorators: Richard Pefferle, Jack Moore, Keogh Gleason, Henry Grace, and many others. It was through their combined vision that the Yellow Brick Road took shape, though Moore claimed personal authorship over the poppy field where Dorothy and friends fell asleep. From the memorable little swirl from which it begins—not described in Baum's book—to the rolling, writhing journey it makes through Oz, the Yellow Brick Road charted a path of dreams. Generations of children have followed it in the more than sixty years since it first appeared on the screen.

The whole look of Oz was, in fact, a labor of gay talent: costume designer Adrian created the look of the Munchkins, who danced alongside the road, as well as the fabulous gown worn by Glinda the Good Witch, the outrageous garb of the Wizard's many disguises, and the somehow believable Lion suit worn by Bert Lahr. The entire design of the picture was overseen by Cedric Gibbons, the studio's head art director, who many believed was discreetly homosexual himself. But it is the Yellow Brick Road, the creation of MGM's all-gay decorating unit, that endures as the film's most potent symbol, an iconic cultural image of the world that awaits beyond.

83

Wonder Woman

"In her satin tights, fighting for her rights—and the glory of the red, white, and blue!" So went the campy theme song to the 1970s television show starring Lynda Carter, a fondly remembered childhood pastime for many gay men and lesbians. Indeed, Wonder Woman's various incarnations have been shaped by more gay influences than any other superhero.

A lesbian-feminist icon, Wonder Woman was molded from clay by her mother without the need of any patriarchy. She is Diana, leader of the powerful, noble, altruistic Amazons, sent to man's world to kick it into shape. She was the creation of William Moulton Marston, a Harvard-trained psychologist who was also the inventor of the polygraph—ever wonder where the idea of WW's truth-telling magic lasso came from? In 1941, Marston used the pen name Charles Moulton to create the first great female comic book hero, and to circulate his radical feminist notions. He believed in the coming age of "American matriarchy" in which "women would take over the rule of the country, politically and economically."

Such revolutionary thinking was part of an unconventional lifestyle that Marston led with his alternative family: his wife and a female lover, both of whom bore him children and all of whom lived together in one house. One friend told Wonder Woman biographer Les Daniels that Marston had a "lovely bunch of kids from different wives . . . all living together like one big family—everybody very happy and all good, decent people." Other reports said that Marston also had male lovers: he was an iconoclast in love and politics, and it comes through in his creation.

Various gay artists and writers worked on the *Wonder Woman* comic books, as well as the television show, throughout the ensuing decades. From 2000 to 2003, openly gay artist-writer Phil Jimenez took over the series, for what many believe was one of the Amazon's finest epochs. With great care and love for the characters and their histories, Jimenez helped bring the Wonder Woman mythos into the new millennium.

84

The Hours

Michael Cunningham's Pulitzer Prize–winning novel, inspired by Virginia Woolf's *Mrs. Dallaway,* will go down as one of the great books of all time. Woolf's work is daunting even to the most literary-minded readers, but Cunningham took the themes of loneliness and connection and brilliantly updated them in *The Hours.* It is truly one of the great literary achievements of the late twentieth century.

Cunningham tells three intertwining stories in the novel. A contemporary woman, Clarissa, is dealing with a friend's illness and ultimate death from AIDS, and in the course of it is forced to consider the concepts of love, friendship, hope, and despair. These ideas are also echoed in the complementary narratives of Woolf's last days and her struggle with depression, and the story of Laura, a 1950s American housewife who yearns to find someplace where she belongs.

Great literature is that which makes us wonder about life, that prompts us to reconsider what we've presumed, that offers us a glimpse into our existence: *There's just this for consolation,* Cunningham writes.

An hour here or there when our lives seem, against all odds and expectations, to burst open and give us everything we've ever imagined.

It is that singular insight into the human condition that makes the work so timeless. It's no surprise that a major Hollywood film was made from Cunningham's work, attracting top stars like Meryl Streep, Julianne Moore, and Nicole Kidman (who'd win an Academy Award for her performance as Virginia Woolf). As lovely as the film is, however, it could not hope to fully embody the profound beauty of the novel; *The Hours* is not easily put onto film. It is meant to be read, savored; it is not meant to be easily consumed. Like Woolf, it can be dense and difficult, but in that very struggle lies its power.

85

Dance Music

When I was a kid, I witnessed the backlash against disco. It was too gay, the cool older boys declared, settling on punk as a much preferred alternative. Later, when disco—now known more generically as "dance music"—attempted something of a comeback in the early 1990s (the days of C&C Music Factory, Black Box, Real McCoy, etc.) it decried the gay connotation. "Dance music isn't gay," more than one artist insisted, with some top names (Freedom Williams, Marky Mark) making obligatory homophobic remarks just to make sure the point got across.

But let's face it: dance music *is* gay—very gay. Sylvester, who ruled the dance floors of the 1970s with his powerhouse tracks, was one mighty real queen. The Village People were a big gay in-joke foisted on an unsuspecting public. So many of the great promoters of the big dance clubs of the era were gay. Mel Cheren was called the "godfather of disco," and as a founder of the influential West End Records, he deserves the title. Cheren was present at the very creation of disco, with his ex-lover Michael Brody creating the legendary Paradise Garage disco in

New York City. Rivaled only by Studio 54 (where owner Steve Rubell was also gay), the Garage inspired both technical and social innovations that changed the music industry.

That legacy lives on in the magnificent circuit parties—a uniquely gay phenomenon that celebrates hedonism and community spirit—where dance music has evolved into a diverse range of styles, tempos, and textures. The parties of Jeffrey Sanker and other promoters have allowed for the emergence of DJs not only as record-spinners but as true, individual artists: Manny Lehman, Brett Henrichsen, Abel, Julian Marsh, Victor Calderone, Peter Rohafer, Junior Vasquez, and many others.

In Europe, dance music is a vital part of the popular music scene, played as often on radio as rock or rap or any other form. In North America, in large part because of the hostility toward the gay influences on the genre, dance music remains ghettoized. Yet it remains a powerful and vibrant part of the music scene, for which we can justifiably be proud.

86

The Bride of Frankenstein

James Whale's masterpiece is regularly considered one of the greatest films ever made. Too funny and camp to be an outright horror film, too scary and poignant to be easily labeled a black comedy, *The Bride of Frankenstein* is unique unto itself—the mark of all great films.

Whale had directed the original *Frankenstein* in 1931 for Universal, making Boris Karloff a star and forever shaping Mary Shelley's tale of the modern Prometheus in the popular culture mind. It is a beautiful, lyrical film, from Karloff's pathetic attempt to grasp rays of sunlight in his hands to the heartbreaking scene of the little girl drowning. It is evidence of Whale's brilliant, highly individual filmmaking.

Yet even more so than the original, *The Bride of Frankenstein* (1935) is Whale's greatest achievement as an iconoclastic artist. This is not just a rendering of Shelley's tale, or simply a reworking of events to provide an eager studio with a sequel to a profitable film. Rather, Whale used the bare bones of the Frankenstein story to craft his own tale of life and death, using the monster and his mate as metaphors for good and evil, light and dark. It is such a rich, compelling picture that one never grows tired of watching it; there is always something new to observe, to appreciate, to discover. The monster's rampage through the cemetery, where he is captured and strung up on a post, Christ-like; the quiet interlude with the blind hermit, where Whale had the sheer audacious brilliance to layer on a few chords of "Ave Maria"; the quirky scene of the little people in Dr. Pretorius's jars, one of whom, a randy King Henry VIII, escapes and must be captured with a pair of tweezers.

There is, quite simply, nothing else like it. Whale, undisguised about his own gayness, brought a distinct queer sensibility to the film, from the arch campiness of Ernest Thesiger's Pretorius to the notion that two men, without the need of a woman, will create life. Most memorable of all, of course, is Elsa Lanchester's hissy fit as the monster's mate, endlessly parodied for the last fifty years—a sign of a truly great work of art.

87

Mae West

Without gay men, there would be no Mae West. The point could be argued for other great gay icons as well: gay men have helped shape the images and careers of divas from Theda Bara, Joan Crawford, and Judy Garland to Marilyn, Madonna, and Britney Spears. But nowhere is it more apparent than in the case of Mae West, who from her first steps onto a vaudeville stage in the early twentieth century was paying tribute to the gay subculture that so fascinated and influenced her.

Mae's original act was shaped by the sassy, wisecracking drag queen Bert Savoy, one of the most popular acts in vaudeville. Savoy's writer, Thomas Gray, would write much of Mae's material. She honed her act around Savoy's personality (coupled with that of the great diva, Eva Tanguay), which prompted more than one critic to speculate that Mae West was, in reality, a drag queen.

Certainly her persona was defined by the culture of gay male camp, which she was constantly mining for material, as evidenced in both her breakout stage shows, *Sex* and *The Drag*. She always surrounded herself with gay men, from writers to costumers to publicists, and they helped shape the phenomenon we know as Mae West.

West shook up the culture's notions about sex. She boldly claimed a public expression for women's sexuality that had never been seen before. One of the most influential figures in pop culture of all time, West owed her mystique to gay men, something she was never adverse to pointing out: "I learned it all from the gay boys."

88

Song of Myself

One of the most beautiful poems of all time, written by the Great Gay (er, Gray) Poet himself, Walt Whitman:

> *I celebrate myself, and sing myself,*
> *And what I assume you shall assume,*
> *For every atom belonging to me as good belongs to you.*

Elegantly lyrical, "Song of Myself" offers an unself-conscious exploration of the American experience. While Whitman's poetry is often characterized by what critics have called a celebration of "shared identity," this one stands out as perhaps the most evocative expression of the connection among humanity, God, and country. It's not a routinely patriotic ode, but rather a heartfelt rendition of what it means to belong to a nation, to a community, to a collective spirit.

Whitman began writing *Leaves of Grass,* of which "Song of Myself" is a part, in late 1854. The definitive edition was finally published in

1881. As a poet, Whitman could be uneven, but he shone brilliantly when he examined those "smallest sights and hearings," when he illuminated the minutiae of everyday life. His "Calamus" poems have been called the most extraordinary literary paeans to male love ever written.

His greatest poem remains "Song of Myself," taught now in nearly every high school, most American children's first exposure to literary poetry. Whitman's special awareness of life around him comes alive through his words, encouraging his readers, even more than a century later, to rediscover their own love of life and creation:

> *I bequeath myself to the dirt to grow from the grass I love,*
> *If you want me again look for me under your bootsoles.*
> *You will hardly know who I am or what I mean,*
> *But I shall be good health to you nevertheless,*
> *And filter and fibre your blood.*
> *Failing to fetch me at first keep encouraged,*
> *Missing me one place search another,*
> *I stop somewhere waiting for you.*

89

Dorothy Arzner

In the heyday of the great movie studios, only one woman rose up the ranks to become a director: Dorothy Arzner, who defied all the rules—from dressing like a man to making movies where the woman wasn't always cast in subservient roles.

Starting out as a film editor in the 1910s, Arzner hit her stride as a director of Clara Bow pictures, surprising the brass at Paramount with her skill and sharp eye. By the 1930s the novelty of a female director was played out in the fan magazines, with Arzner always turning up with her mannish short haircut and wearing a suit and tie. Sharing her home with her longtime (fifty years) lover, choreographer Marion Morgan, Arzner was a maverick, eschewing Hollywood studio publicity and always charting her own course.

That independence is reflected in her films. Dismissed by many male critics at the time, Arzner's films today hold up refreshingly well, offering a subtle feminist spin that defies the usual Hollywood studio product. Her heroines—Clara Bow, Katharine Hepburn, Rosalind Russell—exist on their own, not defined in relation to their leading men. It is not surprising that Arzner's best films are those on which she collaborated with Zoe Akins, a screenwriter who also shared her home and her life with a woman.

The Wild Party, Working Girls, Merrily We Go to Hell, Christopher Strong, Craig's Wife, and several others—these films should be revived more often and shown at gay or feminist film festivals. For Arzner was truly an original: the lone woman working in a field dominated by men, she crafted stories with a decidedly different perspective. What seemed odd in 1935 today feels modern and relevant.

90

Camp

It's one of gay culture's great gifts to the world—from the writings of Oscar Wilde to the shenanigans of the Fab Five—but just what *is* camp? Susan Sontag has written: *Many things in the world have not been named; and many things, even if they have been named, have never been described. One of these is the sensibility—unmistakably modern, a variant of sophistication but hardly identical with it—that goes by the cult name of Camp.*

She went on to make an attempt at describing it: *Indeed the essence of Camp is its love of the unnatural: of artifice and exaggeration. And Camp is esoteric—something of a private code, a badge of identity even, among small urban cliques.* But she'd acknowledge: *To talk about Camp is therefore to betray it. No one who wholeheartedly shares in a given sensibility can analyze it; he can only, whatever his intention, exhibit it. To name a sensibility, to draw its contours and to recount its history, requires a deep sympathy modified by revulsion.*

While camp has been adopted by straight artists and writers and even just everyday Joe Schmos, it is, undeniably, an outgrowth of gay urban subculture, where the mocking, critical, outside observer status allowed the sensibility to take hold and develop. Even expressions of camp sensibility that predate the forming of self-conscious gay communities—the operas of Bellini, for example—have been recognized as camp retroactively and reclaimed by gay culture.

Probably the best way to define camp is to give examples of it: Mae West self-consciously mimicking and exaggerating the sexual traits of a vamp. The drawings of Aubrey Beardsley. Bette Davis bulging her eyes and exclaiming to Joan Crawford, "But ya ah in that chair!" Jack and Karen trading barbs on *Will and Grace.* The novels of Ronald Firbank. The girls on *Sex in the City* talking about the size of their boyfriends' penises. And, as Sontag wrote astutely: *stag movies seen without lust.*

The whole point of camp is to dethrone the serious, Sontag concluded. And that to me is one very good reason for pride.

91

Interior Design

Okay, so it's one of the oldest stereotypes in the book. But most stereotypes reflect some truth, and in this case, it's more true than usual. Gay men and lesbians did indeed create and shape the art of interior design. What's surprising is that I should have reversed that phrase, since it was the women—not the men, who are more usually identified with the image of "interior decorator"—who really led the way.

Elsie de Wolfe, later to be Lady Mendl, practically invented interior decorating in the late nineteenth century. Certainly she is called the "first professional interior designer," legendary for her introduction of light colors and casual decor into formerly dark and heavy Victorian-era settings. Despite her late-in-life marriage to Lord Mendl (her friend, gay director George Cukor, quipped she was in it "simply for the title"), Wolfe was the longtime lover of powerful theatrical agent Elisabeth Marbury.

One of Elsie's contemporaries and acquaintances, Julia Morgan, was another influential lesbian on the development of twentieth-century interior design. Morgan was the first woman registered as an architect in California, and her work was as brilliant as it was eclectic. Her most famous work, the Hearst Castle at San Simeon, is a varied mix of European and American elements. Critic Sara Boutelle observed that Morgan created "sumptuous designs that flaunted a hedonism startling for so modest an architect." Morgan would go on to design more than seven hundred buildings.

Influenced by both de Wolfe and Morgan was their friend, William Haines (see p. 161), who set the tone for 1930s and '40s Los Angeles design. By this time, most of the preeminent interior designers in America were gay: Tony Duquette, Tom Douglas, Ted Graber (who redesigned the White House for Nancy Reagan), Billy Baldwin, and so many others. The very *look* of America for much of the past century was largely the vision of gay and lesbian designers.

92

Six Feet Under

It's just the best damn show on television, that's all. Created by openly gay Alan Ball (also the producer-writer of the acclaimed *American Beauty*), *Six Feet Under* follows the ups and downs of the eccentric, dysfunctional, but always loving Fisher funeral home clan. There's quirky mom, Ruth, perennially jumping from relationship to relationship, trying to find some tonic for her unceasing loneliness; hunky eldest son Nate, and his on-again, off-again romance with the strange but fascinating Brenda; middle son David, who blossoms from closet case to full-fledged member of the Los Angeles Gay Men's Chorus; and the brilliant, conflicted, ironic, caustic daughter Claire, who delivers the best lines of the show.

Each episode begins with another death—the corpse of which winds up at Fisher & Sons Funeral Parlor—reminding us, as the show's tagline says, that our whole lives are leading up to this. Few shows have ever treated death so honestly, as much a part of life as anything else. When Claire laments, "Why do people have to die?" Nate responds: "To make life important."

Ball has created a series (he also writes and directs various episodes) in which we care about the characters, so much so that we think about them between shows, wonder what they're doing, how they might respond to events. The emotions are real: when Lisa was found dead this past season, I grieved as if I'd lost a real friend. This is the potential of good drama: like good literature, the characters become real when the emotion is authentic, not contrived.

And what characters they are! I love it when I see Joanna Cassidy's name in the opening credits, knowing that Brenda's loopy mother is going to make an appearance. Claire has had a succession of creepy boyfriends, all of whom have left memorable imprints. (Remember when she stole that foot from the freezer and put it in Gabe's locker?) The actors are letter-perfect in their parts: Frances Conroy as Ruth, Peter Krause as Nate, Michael C. Hall as David, Rachel Griffiths as Brenda, and Lauren Ambrose as Claire. David's relationship with Keith (Matthew St. Patrick) may be a bit dysfunctional, but it's the most honest depiction of a gay relationship in the history of popular entertainment. Just as it isn't unusual to see Nate and Brenda having sex, so too do David and Keith get it on. It's all a part of life.

Life and death. That's what the show is about. Best damn show on television. Period.

93

Disney

Fact is, old Uncle Walt was a right-wing ideologue, and if he were still running the show, we'd never have seen such wonderful flights of fancy as *The Lion King, Beauty and the Beast, Mulan,* or even *Lilo and Stitch.* We certainly wouldn't have seen Disney become one of the leaders in gay rights, becoming one of the first companies in the nation to extend domestic partnership benefits to its employees. And we certainly wouldn't have seen its theme parks conceived, designed, and maintained with what is clearly a definite gay sensibility at work.

So what can this enlightenment be attributed to? The thousands of gay and lesbian employees throughout the vast Disney enterprise, who have succeeded in remaking "the Mouse" into one of the most welcoming environments in the nation. Sure, they don't officially endorse (wink-wink) the June "Gay Days" at the Magic Kingdom, but with so many gay "cast members" working in the parks it was bound to become one of the most popular events of the year. Even during the so-called "non-gay" days, the Magic Kingdom, Epcot, Disney-MGM, and Animal

Kingdom—not to mention the venerable old Disneyland in California—are about as gay as you can get.

I remember meeting a couple of gay Disney employees a few years ago who insisted that I check out the Tiki Birds exhibit. The Tiki Birds? I was aghast. I remembered that dreadful experience from the time I'd been to the park as a kid with my parents. No way would I sit through it again. But the cast members coaxed me in anyway, assuring me it had been done over. Indeed it had—now, instead of a bunch of ceramic and stuffed birds singing inane little tunes, a wisecracking, very Paul Lyndesque toucan tells them all to shut up and takes over the show. A wonderful primer in Gay Sensibility 101.

It just goes to show what we can do when enough of us get together to remake an attraction—or an entire company—in our image. Bravo.

94

Provincetown

It's a place of rare beauty and special magic, that little stretch of sand at the end of the road. Provincetown—its sunlight reflecting off the water in three directions, transfixing generations with its peculiar, transcendent light. Provincetown, at the very tip of Cape Cod—a place that is home away from home for so many gay men and lesbians, who have been part of the artsy, bohemian mix for more than one hundred years.

The first gay communities of Provincetown arrived with the establishment, in the 1890s, of the art colony of painters and sculptors. By the 1910s, it had also become a place for many New York writers to find a summer haven, and the eclectic mix of poets, playwrights, and visual artists produced a vibrant, provocative community. Throughout the decades a diverse assortment of gay and lesbian artists created some of their greatest works in Provincetown: Charles Demuth, Marsden Hartley, Maud Squires, Ethel Mars, Tennessee Williams, Edna St. Vincent Millay, Gore Vidal, Andy Warhol, John Waters.

Before Stonewall, Provincetown was one of the few safe havens for gay people in America. Much of the entertainment has always had an alternative twist: Gore Vidal recalls sneaking none other than Jackie Kennedy in to see a lesbian comic show at the Moors. Famed impressionists Charles Pierce, Craig Russell, and Jim Bailey all became Provincetown regulars in the 1960s, and Andy Warhol discovery Holly Woodlawn performed for several summers. Wayland Flowers (with his tart-tongued puppet Madame) was a leading draw for many years. Paul Lynde, Lily Tomlin, Jimmy James, Kate Clinton, Lea Delaria, Ryan Landry, Varla Jean Merman, and so many others have left their imprint on Provincetown's entertainment scene.

Today Provincetown is a safe, gay-friendly town where you can be open and carefree: the local business guild calls it "the world as it should be," and so it is. Here you can be more yourself than just about anywhere else in the world. Walk hand-in-hand with your lover along Commercial Street, dazzled by the street theater. Friends are made easily and quickly—if you've come to Provincetown single, chances are you won't go home that way.

95

Bayard Rustin

For more than half a century, Bayard Rustin was a leader in the struggle for human rights and economic justice. His first work came with the Brotherhood of Sleeping Car Porters, the premier black trade union, and with the Fellowship of Reconciliation (FOR), touring the country to promote racial cooperation. In 1942 he advocated for the rights of Japanese Americans imprisoned in internment camps.

After the war (during which he spent part of the time in prison for his refusal to serve) Rustin helped plan the first "freedom ride" in the South, challenging Jim Crow practices. Known as the "Journey of Reconciliation," riders engaged in direct protest by intentionally violating the segregated seating patterns on Southern buses and trains. Along the way, they were beaten, arrested, and fined. Arrested in North Carolina, Rustin was put to work on a chain gang. His account of that experience, serialized in the *New York Post,* spurred an investigation that contributed to the abolition of chain gangs in North Carolina.

Rustin was influential in convincing President Truman to abolish segregation in the armed forces. Later, he worked with Martin Luther King Jr. in the early days of the Montgomery bus boycott. Rustin's experience in the theory, strategies, and tactics of nonviolent direct action and civil disobedience greatly influenced King.

It wasn't just civil rights that Rustin advocated; he was also active in labor causes, refugee issues, and foreign policy, leading the American charge against apartheid in South Africa and British colonialism in India. As chairman of the executive committee of Freedom House, an agency that monitors international freedom and human rights, Rustin observed elections in Zimbabwe, El Salvador, and Grenada. His last mission abroad, coordinated by Freedom House, was a delegation to Haiti to help create democratic reform in that country.

As a gay man, he was remarkably open for his time. His gayness often relegated him to a behind-the-scenes role in various campaigns and eventually cost him his job at FOR. But he saw the connections between oppression, and did not hide one part of himself so that the rest of him might be more tolerable to the mainstream. He stands as one of the most extraordinary figures of courage and integrity of the twentieth century.

96

The Fab Five

Watching *Queer Eye for the Straight Guy,* my sister turned to me and said, "See, this proves everybody can get along." A simple enough statement, and yet quite profound. How many straight girls like my sister watch this show, then turn to their husbands or boyfriends and tell them to "get over" their homophobia? When a straight guys hugs one of the Fab Five, it's doing more to end two hundred years of fear and prejudice than any other show on TV.

So there's good reason to love *Queer Eye.* Plus, there's Kyan. Okay, I'll admit it. I haven't had a crush on a TV star like this since David Cassidy.

Of course there are four others besides grooming guru Kyan Douglas: design doctor Thom Filica, fashion savant Carson Kressley, food and wine connoisseur Ted Allen, and culture vulture Jai Rodriguez. Determined to clue up the cluttered and confused straight world, each week the guys transform some dowdy straight man into a Prince Charming. The series was created by David Collins, a gay man, and developed by David Metzler, a straight man—a fusion of energy that gives the show its edge. It's a complete lifestyle makeover, in which straight guys turn in their pleats for flat fronts, learn about wines that don't come in a jug, and come to understand just why hand soap is not a good shampoo (and vice versa).

Each of the five guys is a terrific ambassador from Gaydom to Heteroland. Sure, there's been sniping in the gay press about how they're just a bunch of fairy godfathers or court jesters, whose only function is to entertain the straights. Please: lighten up and enjoy the show. Not one of the Five is a simpering lapdog. They are confident and assured: this is the image for out gay celebrities to follow. Even Carson, who some (again in the gay press) decried for being a stereotypical queen: sure he is, and he's fun. I love queens. He's who he is, and nobody's going to make him act any differently.

So here are the reasons to love the Fab Five: Kyan. Ending prejudice. Laughter. Kyan. Challenging assumptions. Making friends. Grooming tips. And did I mention Kyan?

97

Gordon Merrick

The first gay book I ever read was *The Lord Won't Mind*. Even the title was affirming. And the drawing on the cover, of two handsome, studly, masculine guys obviously in lust for each other, excited my budding teenage libido in ways I didn't know were possible. It took weeks to get the courage to buy it from my local Waldenbooks, but I devoured it under my sheets at home, carefully hiding it from my parents under lock and key in a strong box I'd bought just for that purpose.

Gordon Merrick was a gay Jackie Collins or Danielle Steel. And amazingly, his books were *New York Times* best sellers more than thirty years ago, the first evidence of the buying strength of the gay market. For these weren't beat-around-the-bush (I know, bad pun) kinds of books: these were explicit, if often turgid and stereotypical, gay male romances. They had this kid in thrall.

The Great Urge Downward (my candidate for greatest title of a gay book for all time), *An Idol for Others*, *The Quirk*, *Perfect Freedom*, *Now Let's Talk About Music*, and the Peter and Charlie trilogy: *Forth into*

Light, The Lord Won't Mind, and *One for the Gods.* These are just some of Merrick's titles that helped give a generation a face and a voice.

Merrick attended Princeton but did not graduate, dropping out of school to try acting in New York before turning to writing. His early novels are more mainstream, although often with significant gay subplots. He left America after serving in World War II, dividing his time between France and Sri Lanka. He died in 1988.

When *The Lord Won't Mind* spent several weeks on the best seller list in 1970, one reviewer for the newspaper opined that it "would set homosexuality back at least twenty years." In truth, Merrick's books—potboilers that they were—did just the opposite. At a time when homosexuality in literature was still largely treated as a closet identity that could only end in tragedy, Merrick wrote with celebration (and juicy details) about gay relationships that ended happily. His books anticipated the rise of the Violet Quill writers and a self-affirming gay literature by the end of the decade. And they made a generation of adolescents like myself giddily aware that we weren't the only ones in the world with that great urge downward—and that, ultimately, the Lord wouldn't mind.

98

Tyron Garner and
John Geddes Lawrence

Don't know those names? Two words: sodomy decision. The year 2003 was a big one: the United States Supreme Court overruled *Bowers v. Hardwick*, which allowed states to continue criminalizing gay sex. Then the Massachusetts Supreme Court ordered the state to extend marriage rights to gay people, a decision some are still trying to thwart as we go to press. But no one can change *Lawrence et al. v. Texas*, the decision that struck down the nation's sodomy laws. And while many dedicated lawyers fought for that victory, it was the courage and integrity of two men who made it possible: Tyron Garner and John Geddes Lawrence.

In 1998—not 1938, not 1958, but 1998—Houston police broke into an apartment on a false alarm and found the two men having sex. Private, consensual, in their own apartment—but they were arrested and fined $200 under the Texas anti-sodomy law. How many others, more fearful, less self-aware, have simply paid the fine and slunk away, ashamed and mortified, as the system wanted them to be? Not Garner and Lawrence, who fought the indignity on their lives and their love all the way up to the U.S. Supreme Court. And they won.

There was much hoopla over the Court's decision: *Newsweek* proclaimed that it would "change forever the status of homosexuals in America." Justice Anthony Kennedy declared, in wording that surprised court watchers with its breadth and reach, that gay people "are entitled to respect for their private lives." The state cannot demean their existence or control their destiny by making their private sexual conduct a crime.

The right fulminated and frothed at the mouth, surely part of the rage that is fueling the anti-marriage battle in Massachusetts. But with jubilation and dignity did Garner and Lawrence receive the news. Though it will be many years before the full impact of *Lawrence* is felt in gay marriage, gay adoption, or gays in the military (after all, it took decades for *Brown v. Board of Education* to end segregation), the decision of two ordinary men in Texas to stand up for themselves will resound forever in history.

99

GLAD

Founded in 1978, Gay & Lesbian Advocates & Defenders (GLAD) is New England's leading legal rights organization dedicated to ending discrimination based on sexual orientation, HIV status, and gender identity and expression. And it is due to their ingenuity and dedication that the Supreme Judicial Court of Massachusetts, on November 18, 2003, ruled in *Goodridge v. Dept. of Public Health* that same-sex couples have a right to marry in Massachusetts.

Providing litigation, advocacy, and educational work in all areas of gay rights, GLAD has a full-time legal staff and a network of cooperating attorneys across New England, all of whom are worthy of our pride. But it is Mary Bonauto, GLAD's Civil Rights Project director, who has emerged as one of the great heroes of our times. Bonauto has proven that the law can indeed be used as a tool for good, that it can be made to work for us, not against us. In 1999, Bonauto was instrumental in helping to secure the Vermont ruling that declared same-sex couples entitled to all the same benefits and protections of civil marriage. It led the way to Vermont's historic civil union law, and certainly influenced the Massachusetts court decision, for which Bonauto also worked tirelessly.

"When we go to court," GLAD says in its public statement, "we go there to win." But regardless of the outcome, each time they take on a case, they are sending a message and chipping away at outdated laws.

GLAD goes on to say: "The commitment to individual dignity and freedom is an intrinsic part of the American experience, yet for many of us, the way we are treated by society reflects a very different reality." Now in its twenty-fifth year of fighting for our legal rights, GLAD has helped shape American society, often with much resistance, to be in alignment with its founding principles: that all people are created equal and endowed with certain inalienable rights.

100

Mel Boozer

People make a big deal—and with reason—about all the gay visibility at the Democratic National Convention of 1992. But in doing so, they often forget that one man had already blazed that path twelve years before, when Mel Boozer was the first openly gay delegate to address a national convention.

An African American man from the District of Columbia, Boozer was president of the Gay Activists Alliance and was running a symbolic campaign for the vice presidency. He's become a legendary figure in the District, where residents remember him for his activism there, including his fight for the Sexual Assault Reform Act that overturned DC's sodomy law (reinstated by Congress later, sadly, after pressure from Jerry Falwell). But Boozer should be acclaimed beyond the District as well. Here's what he said at the convention in 1980:

"I rise in thankful recognition of the citizens of the District of Columbia who voted for me to come here knowing that I am gay. I rise in anguished recognition of more than twenty million Americans who love this country and who long to serve this country in the same freedom that others take for granted, twenty million lesbian and gay Americans whose lives are blighted by a veil of ignorance and misunderstanding. . . .

"We come from towns and cities where our friends are jailed and beaten on the slightest pretext. We come from churches which have been burned to the ground because they admit us to worship. We come from families which have been torn apart because we have lost our jobs, and we have lost our good names which have been slandered by false accusations, myths, and lies. . . .

"Would you ask me how I'd dare to compare the civil rights struggle with the struggle for lesbian and gay rights? I can compare, and I do compare them. I know what it means to be called a nigger. I know what it means to be called a faggot. And I can sum up the difference in one word: none."

Extraordinary words that deserve to be remembered. As does the man who spoke them. Mel Boozer died of AIDS in 1987.

101

Some Guy in Nebraska . . .

. . . and some gal in Mississippi. You know who I mean. We all know folks like the ones I'm talking about, people who live lives of quiet integrity and inauspicious dignity. People who don't hide who they are, who go to work and live in their communities without pretending, without lying, without making apologies. They are the real reasons for pride, for they are the ones who are changing the world.

So, for discussion, let's call this guy in Nebraska "Hank." He runs a small business in a small town, and for the past twenty years, he's kept a photo of his longtime partner (let's call him "Frank") where his customers can see it. If they ask who it is—and they often do—he tells them, "My other half." That's it: no political speeches, no diatribes. "My other half" says it all.

People love Hank in that community. They've all known him for years, and they know him to be a good citizen, a good neighbor, a good friend. He can jaw with the best of them, crack a joke and offer advice on how to best barbeque spareribs. He's never been strident, never been obnoxious—he's just been himself, year in and year out, showing up with Frank to local spaghetti suppers, hanging up a shamrock for St. Patrick's Day in March and a rainbow flag in June.

That young lady in Mississippi offers a similar tale. We can call her "Velma." She's just sixteen, but already she's standing up for herself, living more authentically than many others decades older than she ever manage to do. Yet, like Hank, Velma doesn't see herself as an activist for change. She's just living her life, getting ready to take a girl to her junior prom, even asking her mom to iron her brother's powder-blue tuxedo so she can wear it. Velma wants to be a veterinarian, and she sees no reason why she and a girlfriend—this one or another—can't someday get married. Like so many gay and lesbian youths, she's forging ahead into the future on her terms. She's not trying to keep up with the world; the world is going to have to catch up with her.

When I look at how far the gay movement has come, when I consider how much farther along it will be in ten years, I know that the reasons for that progress are people like Hank and Velma. Above everything else—above all the art and culture and politics and science—what I remain most proud of are the everyday men and women who live authentically and without apology. Multiply Hank and Velma a hundred thousandfold and you'll get the picture—and with the inexorable march of youth, that number is only going to continue to grow. The 101st reason for pride? You bet. And the 102nd, 103rd . . . on into infinity.